Guiding Faculty to
EXCELLENCE

Instructional Supervision in the Christian School

Second Edition

Guiding Faculty to EXCELLENCE

Instructional Supervision in the Christian School

Second Edition

Gordon B. Brown, Ed.D.

purposeful design
p u b l i c a t i o n s

Purposeful Design Publications is the publishing division of the Association of Christian Schools International (ACSI) and is committed to the ministry of Christian school education, to enable Christian educators and schools worldwide to effectively prepare students for life. As the publisher of textbooks, trade books, and other educational resources within ACSI, Purposeful Design Publications strives to produce biblically sound materials that reflect Christian scholarship and stewardship and that address the identified needs of Christian schools around the world.

Unless otherwise identified, all Scripture quotations are taken from the New American Standard Bible (NASB), © 1960, 1962, 1963, 1968, 1971, 1972, 1973, 1975, 1977, 1995, 1997 by the Lockman Foundation.

Printed in the United States of America
16 15 14 13 12 11 10 09 08 07   3 4 5 6 7

Brown, Gordon B.
Guiding faculty to excellence: Instructional supervision in the Christian school
    Second edition
    ISBN 978-1-58331-015-1 Catalog #6372

Designer: Thom Hoyman
Editor: Mary Endres

Purposeful Design Publications
A Division of ACSI
PO Box 65130 • Colorado Springs, CO 80962-5130
Customer Service: 800-367-0798 • Website: www.acsi.org

Contents

Often professional literature is written by a practitioner and is practical, but very little of it represents new thinking. The material lacks the benefit of current theory and research. It simply rehearses commonsense and well-worn ideas about the subject. The reader receives a measure of affirmation but minimal stimulation.

On other occasions books are written by a member of the academic community and are research-based and theoretical but lacking in application. You read the material and review the statistics, but you see little relevance to your work as a Christian school administrator. The author clearly hasn't walked in your shoes or sat in your chair.

In *Guiding Faculty to Excellence,* theory and practice on instructional supervision come together seamlessly. After reading this book, you will more keenly understand your responsibilities as a godly supervisor. You will also be better equipped to carry out your task of helping good Christian teachers become better.

Gordon Brown has taught for twelve years in higher education and has regularly taught supervision at the graduate level. His dissertation at the University of Miami (Florida) researched the topic "Leader Behavior and Faculty Cohesiveness in Christian Schools." He is clearly in touch with supervision theory and research. Additionally, Dr. Brown served for nineteen years as a Christian school administrator. He observed classes, evaluated teachers, and entered into staff conferencing to help his Christian faculty grow spiritually and professionally. He has walked in your shoes!

The Christian school movement thanks Dr. Brown for his scholarly effort and spiritual sensitivity in producing this book on instructional supervision.

Robert M. Miller, Ed.D.
ACSI Director of Administrative Leadership Development

My special appreciation and recognition are extended to the following persons who have been instrumental in making this book a reality.

To Steve Babbitt, ACSI's director of publishing services, who extended the initial invitation to pen this second edition of my supervision book, who faithfully exchanged emails and chapter documents with me during the writing process, and who shepherded the manuscript through to its completion and eventual publication. Thank you, Steve, for your partnership in this endeavor.

To Bob Miller, ACSI's leadership development director, who invited me to present supervision principles and practices during spring 2000 to Christian school administrators in 25 cities. It was this series of "One-Day Enablers" that provided the impetus for this book. Thank you, Bob, for inviting me to participate in this ministry.

To 800 Christian school administrators and supervisors who attended "One-Day Enablers" during spring 2000 and who generated questions, ideas, feedback, and input for me during the seminars. Their involvement has contributed to the improvement and refinement of this document. Thank you, administrators, for giving me a true sense of sharing with you in your Christian school ministries.

Why Make Supervision of Instruction a Priority in Christian Schools?

Several years ago, a Christian school administrator enjoyed a professional "high." During a faculty pre-service session, a teacher testified that he actually enjoyed his administrator's classroom observation visits. This unusual and unexpected announcement came from one whose contract renewal had been in serious jeopardy in recent years. In a major turnaround, he was now voicing the pleasure and anticipation he felt when he expected the administrator to visit his class.

What made this teacher's expression of pleasure so special to his administrator? Simply this: Earlier that same administrator had made a personal decision to give instructional supervision a high priority, and now her decision was being rewarded. She had hoped her new priority would produce a noticeable difference in her school, and the fruit was becoming evident. The teacher in question, once the object of numerous parent and student complaints, was overcoming important difficulties and was increasingly able to use effective instructional techniques. Without a doubt, the administrator's commitment of time and energy to supervision was reaping a satisfying harvest.

By giving priority to instructional supervision, administrators bring important benefits to their school. To start with, the school's critical activity, classroom instruction, receives the care it deserves and is no longer an afterthought when problems arise. If the administrator believes that what happens in the classrooms is central to the school's mission, giving primary attention to instructional matters becomes a mandate, not an option. Another benefit is that through thoughtful supervision, the administrator communicates concern for teachers—their well-being and professional development. Finally, by giving proactive attention to supervision, the administrator can ensure that biblical principles of leadership are followed intentionally and not overlooked inadvertently in crisis moments. The Scriptures contain abundant guidelines for shepherding groups of followers so that goals are accomplished in godly fashion. If God is to receive full glory and His work is to be advanced, biblically-rooted supervision is a required practice for Christian schools.

Conversely, failure to give priority attention to instructional supervision may damage the school and its ministry. When a careful supervision plan is lacking, experienced teachers may fail to strive for higher levels of excellence and thus may plateau in an environment of low motivation. Because of inadequate mentoring, beginning teachers will fail to overcome rookie problems. Teachers who do not feel supported may find it easy to leave the school because the grass looks greener elsewhere. Administrators may find that they use more of their time than ever to "put out fires" resulting from classroom problems. Parents may perceive a decline in the quality of the instruction, and on occasion the school may even lose students. Yes, there is a price to pay when instructional supervision receives low priority.

Instructional supervision also represents accountability. Parents hold accountable the school's highest authority, whether board or pastor, for the education of their children. The board or pastor, in turn, holds the administrator accountable. Thus, if the administrator fails to hold the teachers accountable for ongoing improvement of instruction, the chain of accountability is broken. Students suffer. Parents become discontented. The board or pastor receives complaints, and the administrator finds herself in an indefensible position.

Why a Book on Instructional Supervision in Christian Schools?

Several factors provided the impetus for the first edition of this book. Cardinal among them was the fact that secular volumes on supervision fail to address certain variables that Christian school administrators face. To start with, these administrators are Christian. The God they serve, the foundation of truth on which they build, and the philosophy that guides their institutions must occupy a pivotal place in any treatment of instructional supervision. This perspective is generally absent from professional publications that do not assume a Christian world and life view.

Secondly, some Christian school administrators experience serious constraints on the time available for supervision. They are in small schools, or larger schools where they are the only administrator. For them it is irrelevant to speak of a curriculum/instruction specialist on the staff, or an assistant principal for instruction, or department heads. They are asking, How can I fit supervision into my schedule?

And finally, most Christian schools exist as single units, not as parts of larger school systems. The administrator has limited or nonexistent outside help and expertise to call on. She must be the resident expert on supervision.

Both the first and second editions are built on these foundational reasons for a book dedicated specifically to instructional supervision in Christian schools. But why bring out a second edition? Speaking practically, the first edition was out of print. ACSI's supply was exhausted. But there were other compelling reasons for a new edition. In the years since publication of the first edition in

1993, Christian schools have matured professionally, administratively, legally, and spiritually. New questions are being faced, and new horizons of possibility are opening up. It is time to develop instructional supervision policies and practices in more detail and diversity while continuing to apply the biblical principles that drive and define the endeavor.

Christian schools now have more teachers and administrators with extended experience in Christian education, and these people have the ability to make important contributions to the overall instructional programs of the schools. But to be free to do so, they must have leaders who will surround them with supervision structures that are carefully planned and are carried out with grace, excellence, and equity. This second edition, while still providing foundational knowledge for new administrators and new schools, is also intended to help mature schools become even better at instructional supervision.

How Should You Use This Book?

This volume is intended to serve in several capacities. Primarily, it is meant to be a "how to" of instructional supervision in Christian schools. Useful ideas, processes, and forms (both in the book and on an accompanying CD) are included for this purpose. Secondarily, it is hoped that the book will serve a philosophical function, to stimulate readers to further search out God's principles and integrate them creatively into school administrative practice. And finally, the pages of this book are meant to abound with healthy quantities of encouragement for the weary administrator whose well of creative energy may have dried up temporarily.

May God meet every reader at his or her point of need.

A Personal Word

The first edition of this book was written to assist Christian school administrators across the country and even the world. It grew out of a class in principles of supervision that I had taught for several summers. From the interaction and questioning of dedicated students, I recognized that even frontline Christian schools lacked a way to help their administrators with supervision, and that such help would be welcome—hence, the first edition.

Since then (1992) I have continued teaching supervision courses in several graduate schools that enroll Christian school administrators. The questions that these students raised, and our subsequent searches for solutions, have added to the body of knowledge presented in that first edition, which, by 1998, was out of print. As a result, I placed the original text on computer disk and continued to modify it for use in my own classes.

Then, in 1999, ACSI provided the opportunity to present one-day seminars on principles of supervision, in both the United States and Canada. Out of those seminars came an invitation to update the book with a revised edition.

Like the first edition, this book comes with my desire that God be lifted up and that Christian schools be better equipped to produce "fruit that remains." As readers attend to these pages, may they be conscious that they are wrapped in much prayer and a sincere concern that God's will be done in every corner of Christian school activity.

Gordon B. Brown

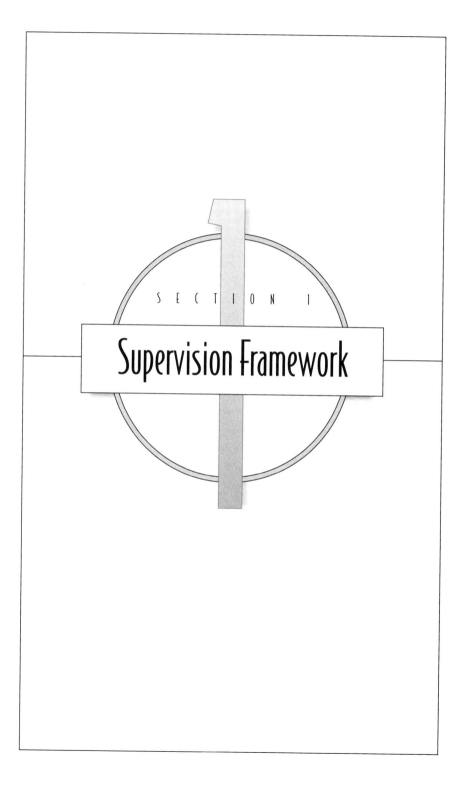

SECTION 1

Supervision Framework

Guiding Faculty to Excellence

1

Biblical Foundations for Supervision

For no man can lay a foundation other than the one which is laid,
which is Jesus Christ.
(1 Corinthians 3:11)

Chapter highlights....

Supervision defined
Biblical principles
An integrative model for this book

A young Christian educator was in her first administrative position. She began her duties with a mixture of enthusiasm and apprehension. She enjoyed students. She enjoyed teachers. She even enjoyed observing classes and making suggestions to teachers for improving their instruction.

Then the day came when she had to submit recommendations for renewal of teacher contracts. Suddenly, her position was not quite as enjoyable. During the school year, she had formed the serious impression that the quality of a certain teacher's work was marginal. Since she believed in top quality, her conscience required her to recommend that the teacher not be invited back for the following year.

To the teacher, the decision appeared precipitous. During the year the administrator had given him ideas for improving his teaching. However, she had never clearly indicated how precarious his position was, and the teacher had never understood that his contract renewal was in jeopardy. After resisting briefly, he agreed to leave the school—but not without serious misunderstandings, hurt feelings, and loss of respect for the administrator.

On the surface it appears the young administrator was guilty of procedural mistakes, but at the root was a failure to translate her philosophy of biblical integration into her administrative practice. Though meaning well, she had overlooked important biblical principles. The very biblical integration she expected of her teachers was lacking in her own approach to leadership. Biblical principles, understood and applied, must form the foundation for effective supervision in the Christian school.

The true story above illustrates the single most serious shortcoming of Christian school administrators in supervising their teachers—failure to put well-intended philosophy into action. This chapter will lay a foundation of biblical principles that are relevant to the administrator-teacher relationship. Linked with each principle are practical applications to Christian school supervision. These applications will be mentioned briefly in this chapter but amplified in later chapters. I'll break ground by defining supervision.

What Is Supervision?

Supervision has been defined variously as a technical service, a leadership service, a set of activities, a position, a process, and a way of relating.[1] These definitions, though diverse, are similar in that they pinpoint the improvement of classroom instruction as the target of supervision.

Ben Harris, author of management texts, defines supervision as the functions of school operation that are directly instruction related and indirectly pupil related. According to Harris, a supervisor's responsibilities include developing curriculum, scheduling, staffing, providing facilities and materials, arranging for in-service education, evaluating, and orienting new staff. In this view, supervision extends to most activities that affect instruction in any way, those activities that directly or indirectly impact the skills and performance of classroom teachers.[2]

By contrast, Marcia Knoll limits supervision to the direct attention that administrators give individual teachers in order to improve classroom instruction. This attention usually includes conferencing, goal setting, observing, and follow-up, but it does not extend to curriculum development, scheduling, or other administrative functions that affect teachers' classroom performance only indirectly.[3]

Carl Glickman defines supervision as "assistance for the improvement of instruction."[4] This definition allows us to view supervision as a function or process rather than a position or title.

For the purposes of this volume, the author has drawn from all these ideas in formulating a definition of supervision. From Harris comes the idea that supervision can be exercised with teachers as a group, through in-service programs for example. From Knoll comes the idea that supervision is working with teachers directly, and from Glickman comes the emphasis on instructional improvement. From all three emerges the focus of supervision—instructional improvement to achieve better student learning. Therefore, supervision will be conceived as activities performed directly with teachers for the purpose of improving their delivery of classroom instruction and, consequently, enhancing student learning.

This definition puts many administrative tasks outside the scope of this discussion, including scheduling, budgeting, developing curriculum, purchasing materials, selecting staff, and fund-raising. These all contribute to classroom performance, but none are part of supervision as defined in this book.

How Do Biblical Principles Form the Foundation of Supervision?

The Scriptures contain precepts about group functioning that apply to school supervision. Christian school administrators supervise teachers who profess faith in Jesus Christ and are indwelt by the Holy Spirit. The biblical principles outlined here are drawn from New Testament instructions addressed primarily to the church. Though the Christian school is not the church, the same principles apply to all believers in the church, in the workplace, in recreation and leisure, and, yes, in the Christian school. The principles are arranged here according to six major themes: authority and order, mutual submission, unity of purpose, relationships, perpetual improvement, and maximum utilization of personnel. Each principle is supported by Scripture and accompanied by suggested applications to Christian school supervision.

Principles of Authority and Order

The authority resident in the Christian school administrator is God ordained. It is positional authority. It grants school administrators the power and calling to exercise leadership and make decisions. Therefore, administrators are expected to take the initiative for instructional improvement by establishing and following orderly procedures for supervision. Mediocre teaching will not improve unless administrators give supervision thoughtful priority and assume responsibility for energizing the improvement. Where there is good supervision, the administrator is likely to have had a part in establishing it. Conversely, if supervision is poor or nonexistent, the administrator must be the one to initiate change.

God also expects those with authority to be ministers for good by nourishing subordinates, providing gentle oversight, and being examples of effective Christian educators. The following principles set forth these standards:

Verses	Biblical Principle	Application
Romans 13:1	Authority is given by God, and persons in authority are ordained by God.	Administrators take seriously their responsibility to ensure that there is good supervision in their schools.
Ephesians 6:5 Titus 2:9 Romans 13:1 1 Peter 2:13, 18	Everyone is to be subject to higher powers and to human ordinances.	Administrators expect those they supervise to obey "ordinances," but they have in place only those that are needed.
Romans 13:4 1 Peter 2:14	Those in authority are to be ministers of God for good.	Administrators understand that their power is for the purpose of serving and advancing the work of God in schools.
1 Peter 5:2–3 Philippians 3:17; 4:9; 2:20	Those in authority are responsible to feed, take oversight, and be examples.	Administrators guide and nourish others while demonstrating professional growth themselves.
1 Timothy 2:1–2	Prayer should be offered for those in authority.	Administrators pray for their superiors and sincerely expect teachers to pray for them.
1 Corinthians 11, 14	Procedures for order should be established and followed.	Administrators ensure that orderly supervision plans are developed and followed.

The authority issue is complex. Should administrators be "command model" leaders who make the most important decisions themselves, perceiving leadership in terms of authority and the right to require obedience?[5] Or is there room for democracy in Christian school supervision? Is it legitimate for individual teachers, who are themselves priests unto God, to be sources of authority? To what extent should Christian organizations use participative management ideas that involve shared decision-making and delegation of authority to subordinates? Do Christian school administrators wrongly abdicate their authority when they employ these practices?

Issues of authority are simplified when biblical principles for leadership are blended in a balanced way. Administrators who function according to a "command model" are displaying only one side of a biblical picture of leadership. On the other side is mutual submission.

Principles of Mutual Submission

"Servant leadership" is a term trumpeted regularly in Christian leadership literature—and rightly so, for it follows the pattern lived out by Jesus Christ. Christian leaders, in addition to wearing mantles of authority, must willingly place themselves in a servant's posture. How can they do this? It starts with a heart attitude that considers others more important than oneself. It continues with the philosophy that leaders, if they are to serve others, must give their subordinates the best leadership and supervision possible. Administrators who fail to do so are rendering disservice rather than service.

When administrators carry out this service in a nonthreatening and supportive manner, they appropriately submit to subordinates. By assisting teachers, being genuinely impartial, and welcoming teacher expertise in making school decisions, administrators manifest servant leadership, a genuine expression of mutual submission. These principles are identified below:

Verses	Biblical Principle	Application
1 Peter 5:5–6 Ephesians 5:21	Humbling oneself before God demands mutual submission among organization members.	School administrators give priority to meeting the needs of their subordinates.
Galatians 5:13	Mutual submission calls for mutual service	Administrators realize that their supervisory role is actually a service to their subordinates
Ephesians 6:9	Masters should render service to employees, not threats.	Administrators foster teacher growth by assisting, not judging.
Philippians 2:14	Do all things without murmuring and disputing.	Administrators are fair and impartial, thus reducing causes for complaint.

To be servant leaders, administrators do not need to abdicate their positional authority by letting teachers make all the decisions and judgments. Teachers would be robbed of needed guidance, organization, and inspiration if administrators became passive or excessively submissive. Rather, administrators should submit to the notion that teachers genuinely need them, serving the teachers through supervision, coordination, support, and guidance. Management, according to Myron Rush, is meeting the needs of people as they work at accomplishing their jobs.[6]

Mutual submission also mandates the rendering of service, not threats, to subordinates. In supervisory practice, this principle translates into encouraging, assisting, and guiding teachers toward improvement. Attempts to motivate teachers by threat of contract nonrenewal are seen as "last-resort" measures.

Mutual submission includes an administrator's willingness to lead by example. Administrators should set the pace in spiritual vitality, professional improvement, honing of instructional skills, and other aspects of Christian school ministry. Teachers ought to see their administrators setting self-improvement goals, taking further graduate training, attending professional conferences, and reading current literature.

By maintaining a good balance between headship and submission, Christian school administrators foster faculty cohesiveness. While carrying out supervisory functions, administrators must give special care to enhancing, not fracturing, the spiritual unity of purpose within their faculties.

Principles of Unity of Purpose

For Christians, the ultimate purpose of any endeavor emanates from God Himself. The Lord told Israel, "You shall be holy for I am holy"(Leviticus 11:45). He did not say, "Be holy because I have told you to be holy." The Christian's reason for holiness transcends obedience; it resides in the very character of God. Out of God's essence flows the purpose of all the ministries and activities Christians undertake in the work of the kingdom. Therefore, the most certain way to maintain unity of purpose is to bring together those whose purpose for life is centered in God. Then the principles listed below can be implemented:

Verses	Biblical Principle	Application
1 Corinthians 1:10	Faculty members should be of the same mind and judgment, with no divisions.	Administrators emphasize spiritual, philosophical, and instructional commonalities.
1 Corinthians 13	All members are to pursue love.	In various ways administrators set examples of Christian love.
1 Corinthians 5:1–13	The purity and honor of the group should be the concern of all.	Administrators plan for and encourage teachers to help each other.

Is it wise for administrators to assemble a faculty of "yes-men," or convergent thinkers, in order to preserve unity? Or should they risk the differences that will almost certainly surface in a faculty that consists of divergent, perhaps creative, thinkers? For the answer we must recall the basis for unity of purpose—God's qualities and character. If faculty members are focused on God, differences among them will strengthen and unify a school rather than fracture it. Out of commitment to God and His character, teachers will pursue love for each other, will seek to have the same mind on foundational issues, and will work to strengthen and encourage each other. They will demonstrate their cohesiveness as they follow the above principles.

Maintaining unity among Christians does not depend on assembling people who are similar in personality, preferences, abilities, and background. God has combined these elements uniquely in each person. Since no one has all the qualities needed for God's work to thrive, it is wise to develop a faculty with varied strengths and viewpoints whose members adhere to the purpose principles stated above.

Can administrators make a difference in the unity of purpose within their faculties? If not, there is little hope for fractured faculties to reunite on their own. Administrators set the tone by emphasizing major points of agreement and lovingly tolerating minor points of disagreement. In addition, administrators structure time and resources in ways that actively encourage teachers to assist each other rather than to be neutral or contentious. Administrators ensure that their faculty meets regularly for prayer and devotional study of God's Word, keeping the focus on the Person from whom all ultimate purpose flows.

Without unity of purpose in Christian schools, supervision cannot be fully effective. There will be little tolerance for individual differences and shortcomings. Teachers may not easily accept supervisory processes because their own goals for teaching are not in agreement. Administrators may misuse supervisory authority, failing to understand its purposes. Under these conditions, the work of God's Spirit in schools will be blunted. Harmonious relationships can flow only when faculty members are spiritually united. Spiritual unity among students and staff will enhance the quality, depth, and effectiveness of an administrator's supervisory activities.

Principles of Relationships

Relationships of trust between administrators and teachers are essential to effective supervision. Even secular leaders and researchers recognize that trust is crucial. If teachers are suspicious or uncertain about a supervisor's motives, they will view supervision as adversarial. Likewise, if administrators doubt that teachers want to improve, they are likely to use supervision for judgment rather than for assistance.

Administrators build trust relationships when they heed the biblical principles charted below. From hearts of genuine love for teachers, administrators should (1) demonstrate interest in the teachers' welfare, (2) encourage mutual care among teachers, (3) be forthright and honest with teachers regarding performance appraisals, and (4) refrain from discussing teachers' difficulties with others. The novice administrator described at the chapter's beginning sabotaged a trust relationship with the teacher by failing to be forthright and honest early in the evaluation process.

Verses	Biblical Principle	Application
Ephesians 4:25	Truthfulness in relationships is important.	Administrators are open with teachers about substandard performance.
Ephesians 4:29 James 4:11 and 5:9	Speech about others should be free of evil and murmuring.	Administrators do not discuss one teacher's difficulties with another teacher.
1 Corinthians 12:25–26	Members should have mutual care for one another.	Administrators foster a team spirit of cooperation and interdependence.
John 13:34 Romans 12:9–10	Love should be the foundation for all relationships and interactions.	Administrators put the welfare of individual teachers ahead of their own emotional and physical comfort.

When trust relationships exist, supervision brings positive results. Teachers respond to improvement suggestions that are delivered in a loving, non-threatening manner, and the principles of perpetual improvement described below can be implemented in a congenial manner.

Principles of Continuous Improvement

Christian school personnel should never be satisfied with existing levels of expertise and performance. Administrators must take the lead in pursuing excellence. The Scriptures clearly instruct believers to press on spiritually just as Christ did. He was not satisfied until He had fulfilled the Father's will completely. For Christian administrators, all areas of life, including professional practice, are spiritual and are subject to the principles of perpetual improvement listed here:

Verses	Biblical Principle	Application
Ephesians 4:12	Members should be continuously trained and built up.	Supervision is aimed at improvement, not judgment.
Galatians 6:1	One who falls should be restored.	Supervision seeks every means possible to assist struggling teachers.
Philippians 3:14	Each member should be continuously pressing for a high goal.	Administrators structure incentives for continuous professional growth of teachers. They exemplify this growth themselves.

If perpetual improvement is the goal, administrators must aim at growth, not judgment, of teachers. In practice, there must be clearly written policies stating that the purpose of supervision will be to improve instruction. Both teachers and administrators must understand that supervisory procedures are to be carried out fairly, consistently, and in an orderly fashion.

A helpful practice for fostering forward-looking improvement is to set annual goals. All who are involved in the school's ministry, beginning with the highest authority, identify desired improvements in their areas of responsibility. Administrators are important links in this process: (1) they assist the authorities over them in setting and monitoring schoolwide goals, (2) they set personal goals for themselves, and (3) they stimulate teachers to identify improvement objectives. Teachers can improve most easily when they are well placed. Therefore, an important key to consistent improvement is the effective placement and utilization of personnel.

Principles of Maximum Personnel Utilization

Part of a supervisor's role is to make full and appropriate use of each teacher's talents and abilities. As supervisors increasingly "know their sheep," they will place them wisely, thereby creating stronger school programs. Making appropriate placement may require redistributing assignments by changing the grade levels or courses of some teachers or even delegating additional tasks. Administrators who endorse the adage that "there are no failures in God's work, only misplacements" will work hard to ensure that their teachers are placed where their gifts and abilities are most likely to reap success.

Making the best use of the available personnel can lead administrators to use teachers creatively, sometimes in quasi-supervisory roles. Strategies such as peer coaching, master teacher assignments, and buddy systems can promote instructional improvement when administrators have limited time for direct supervision.

It is not only teachers who must be optimally fitted into school structures. Administrators too should make maximum use of their time and gifts. The biblical principles below suggest that supervision is a crucial task to which administrators are called, an urgent one that should be given scheduling priority. They must, then, delegate responsibly those tasks that make use of the strengths of teachers and staff members. If administrators attempt to do too much, or if they respond only to the "tyranny of the urgent," they will neglect instructional supervision, giving to other tasks valuable time and energy (spiritual, emotional, physical, mental) that should be reserved for working with teachers.

Verses	Biblical Principle	Application
Philippians 2:19–29	Tasks and responsibilities are to be delegated.	Administrators overcome the temptation to do it all.
1 Corinthians 12:14–24	Each function must be respected as important.	Administrators attend to each individual teacher as if he or she were the only one.
1 Corinthians 12:4–7	The ability, office, and task of each person is to contribute to the common good.	Administrators use the strengths of various teachers to enrich the total instructional program.
Acts 6:1–4	Overseers should give time priority to functions to which they are called.	Administrators schedule their own time for the proper supervision of instruction.

The scriptural principle is clear: God has given gifts to administrators and teachers, and those gifts should be used to the maximum in service for Him. Administrators must carefully evaluate their personal gifts and those of their teachers to determine how to use those gifts in the most effective ways. "A good leader . . . makes sure all of those in his group or organization have an opportunity to use their skills, abilities, and creativity."[7]

Summary: An Integrative Model for This Book

The biblical principles described above form the foundation and integrative superstructure for all supervisory activities. The six fundamental pillars—authority and order, mutual submission, unity of purpose, relationships, perpetual improvement, and maximum personnel utilization—support the practices suggested in this book.

The discussion of supervision has three primary components:
1. Forming the framework for supervision (Chapters 1–5)
2. Developing people involved in supervision (Chapters 6–9)
3. Employing techniques for supervision (Chapters 10–18)

By cross-referencing the six categories of biblical principles and the three supervisory components, you can see a grid. Within its cells are chapters that outline action plans that administrators can use to integrate biblical principles with supervisory theory.

	Framing Structure	Developing People	Using Techniques
Authority and Order	Chapters 2, 3, 4		Chapters 11, 16
Unity of Purpose	Chapter 2		Chapters 16, 17
Mutual Submission	Chapter 5		Chapter 10
Love in Relationships	Chapters 2, 3, 5	Chapter 8	Chapters 10, 12–15
Perpetual Improvement	Chapters 2, 3, 4	Chapters 6–9	Chapters 11–14
Maximum Utilization of Personnel	Chapters 3, 4	Chapters 7, 8	Chapters 16–18

Supervisor's Prayer

Dear Lord, thank you for being the source of all wisdom in knowing how we, your servants, can live and work together for your glory. Thank you for clearly disclosing your will for daily living in your precious Scriptures. Now we ask for courage and determination to follow the precepts you have given, not to please ourselves or to become successful administrators, but that you may receive great honor and that your kingdom work in Christian schools be mightily advanced. In our Savior's name, Amen.

Endnotes

1. Lloyd W. Dull, *Supervision: School Leadership Handbook* (Columbus, OH: Merrill Publishing Co., 1981), 3.
2. Ben Harris, *Supervisory Behavior in Education* (Englewood Cliffs, NJ: Prentice-Hall, 1963), 13–14.
3. Marcia Knoll, *Supervision for Better Instruction* (Englewood Cliffs, NJ: Prentice-Hall, 1987), 3–5.
4. Carl D. Glickman, Stephen P. Gordon, and Jovita M. Ross-Gordon, *Supervision of Instruction: A Developmental Approach* (Boston: Allyn and Bacon, 1998), 8.
5. Lawrence O. Richards and Clyde Hoeldtke, *A Theology of Church Leadership* (Grand Rapids, MI: Zondervan, 1980), 24–26.
6. Myron Rush, *Management: A Biblical Approach* (Wheaton, IL: Victor Books, 1984), 28.
7. Ibid.

2

The School's Supervision Policy

Let all things be done properly and in an orderly manner.
(1 Corinthians 14:40)

Chapter highlights....

Purpose for a supervision policy
Process for developing a policy
Components of a policy
Sample supervision policy

The administrator grumbles as he notices his calendar—board meeting this month and annual teacher evaluations due. He fumbles through his file drawer, wondering, Where are those observation forms? Finally, he finds them under "Administration—Miscellaneous."

The board meeting is just two weeks away, so he dashes off a memo to the teachers informing them that he will be visiting their classes in the next ten days for annual evaluation purposes. He gives them a copy of the form he will be using.

That afternoon a first-year teacher asks to see him privately. "I was hoping we could have discussed this some time ago," the teacher begins. "I'm very insecure about this evaluation. I don't feel as if things are going well in my class."

A little disturbed, the administrator responds, "I apologize for not visiting your class earlier. Things get so hectic in the office. I guess I've been assuming that no news is good news, and that most teachers are finding solutions to any problems they've encountered. I'll try to take the situation into consideration when I prepare your evaluation."

Why Have a Supervision Policy?

The first and most crucial reason for Christian schools to have written policies to guide the supervision of instruction is to ensure that biblical principles will be carefully incorporated into procedures and practices rather than being overlooked, as they were in the anecdote above. God's instructions for relationships among believers can be studied carefully and applied in an orderly manner. Important principles such as maximum use of teachers' abilities, continuous impetus for improvement, and relationships of love and support can become the fabric of which policies are woven, in a true integration of God's Word with administrative practice. As a result, respect and love between supervisors and teachers will characterize the school's culture.

A second reason for having written policies is to ensure that everyone affected will understand the ground rules for supervision. Board members, administrators, and teachers can expect uniformity of treatment. In the absence of stated policies, supervision procedures usually exist only in the minds of administrators, with the result that supervision is carried out according to an administrator's personal standards. These may vacillate, opening the door to confusion, mistrust, and uncertainty on the part of teachers. Written supervision policies help administrators remain accountable, to both superiors and subordinates.

How to Develop a Supervision Policy

In formulating a supervision policy, school leaders should be guided by three key biblical principles. First, they should exercise their God-ordained leadership role and take responsibility for developing a policy that will meet their school's needs. Second, they should invite their personnel to exercise creativity and offer their own insight while policies are being formed. Third, administrators should be sensitive to the needs of their subordinates and the possible impact supervision policies may have on their teachers' performance and sense of well-being.

The most effective way to develop supervision policies is to invite the input of all those who must either administer the policies or live under them. In most schools, this means that board members, administrators, and teachers will contribute suggestions. Board members must be involved because they are responsible for setting the policies by which the school is administered. Administrators are pivotal because they carry out the policies. Teachers are involved because the policies exist for their performance evaluation and professional improvement.

Do administrators forfeit their own leadership role if policies are formed as described, with a broad base of input? Are "mutual submission" principles likely to paint administrators into corners in which they have little space to influence policy formation? Not at all. It is entirely possible for supervisors to exercise leadership according to biblical principles of authority while submitting to the wisdom of others. In fact, Myron Rush notes that leaders' most valuable resources are the creative abilities of their subordinates.[1] Here is an example of a process that schools might follow in developing workable supervision policies acceptable to most of those concerned:

Phase One: Input	Phase Two: Formation	Phase Three: Adoption
1. Need recognition and support 2. Research 3. General input	1. Tentative policy 2. Revision 3. Draft	1. Board approval 2. Explanation to faculty 3. Appreciation expressed

Phase One: Input (collecting the ideas)

1. The administrator recognizes the need for a policy, discusses the need with the board, and receives support to formulate a recommended policy.
2. The administrator gathers numerous ideas by researching appropriate literature and collecting samples of supervision policies from other schools.
3. The administrator requests faculty and board input in the form of open brainstorming. A wide range of opinion is important at this stage.

Phase Two: Formation (shaping the ideas)

1. The administrator prepares a tentative policy, incorporating the best ideas from the research, board and faculty suggestions, and personal convictions.
2. The administrator asks faculty and board members to affirm, or suggest amendments to, the tentative policy.
3. The administrator prepares a final draft of the policy, taking into account meritorious and/or appropriate suggestions.

Phase Three: Adoption (approving the plan)

1. The administrator presents the final draft of the policy to the board or its appropriate subcommittee for approval. Minor revisions, if needed, are made.
2. The administrator then shares the approved policy with the faculty for their information and understanding, expressing appreciation for their contributions.

Such a process permits all concerned parties to bring their opinions to the table in the formative stages, and as a result they are much more likely to "own" the final policy. At the same time, the administrator's role as initiating leader is preserved. Another benefit is that teachers will sense the administrator's and the board's genuine concern for their well-being. They will see that their leaders have no hidden agenda other than to enhance the quality of God's work in their Christian school. They are more apt to identify with, and serve cooperatively under, policies that are developed in this way.

What Components Make Up a Supervision Policy?

According to Ronald Hyman's supervision handbook, there are six questions about supervision that schools must answer:
1. What is the purpose of supervision?
2. Who will supervise teachers?
3. What will be observed, conferred about, evaluated, and reported?
4. What sources of information will be needed in supervision?
5. What criteria will be used in supervising teachers?
6. What is the overall context for faculty supervision?[2]

The answer to the first question will influence the answers to the other five. The objectives of supervision define the parameters within which supervisory plans may operate. In developing supervision policies, schools may find it convenient to use Hyman's list as an outline. Sooner or later, each of those questions must be answered, either in the written policy or through procedures and practices.

This author would like to suggest a slight variation on Hyman's plan for preparing supervision policies. Such policies should give administrators and teachers freedom to apply their professional expertise in developing specific procedures. It is suggested, therefore, that such policies should state (1) the purposes or objectives of supervision, (2) the responsibilities of personnel relative to supervision, (3) the nature of supervisory activities, and (4) guidelines for teacher evaluation with respect to intensive supervision and nonrenewal of contracts. The following diagram depicts the axle-spokes-wheel relationships among the components of supervision policies and the desired outcome—quality teaching and learning.

Purpose of Supervision

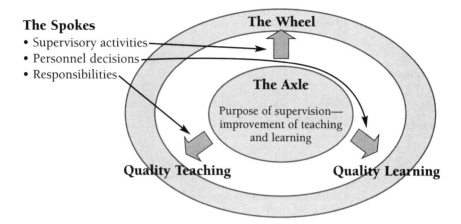

The Spokes
- Supervisory activities
- Personnel decisions
- Responsibilities

The Wheel

The Axle

Purpose of supervision—
improvement of teaching
and learning

Quality Teaching

Quality Learning

By definition, supervision is the body of activities and services that directly impact teachers and their delivery of classroom instruction. Thus, supervision can have only one goal—the improvement of instruction.

This goal is supported by biblical principles pertaining to continuous improvement. In the New Testament church, members were encouraged to press forward to a high calling. When a believer fell into sin, it was the responsibility of others to attempt to restore the fallen one. Even when an erring Christian was removed from church fellowship, it was with the hope that the person would repent (turn toward improvement) and be restored. Accordingly, supervision in Christian schools should be a positive process aimed at developing teachers as instructors.

In practice, however, supervision occasionally looks like "snoopervision," serving only evaluative or judgmental purposes. In such cases, supervisors are likely to visit teachers' classes just before contract renewal time. Their observations then form the bases for conclusive (summative) evaluations of the teachers' performance, allowing administrators to believe they have a substantive case for recommending retention or dismissal.

Ultimately, these two philosophies, improvement and judgment, have a point at which they converge, but that point is not in the statement of supervision's purpose. Supervision's manifest goal should be the growth of teachers and their instructional abilities so that student learning is enhanced. Certainly, evaluation will be an underlying thread throughout that process; the very fact that administrators suggest improvements implies that they first determine a need. But the target of their evaluation must be improvement, not judgment.

Thus, the chief purpose of supervision is not to determine the status of contracts. Administrators who think it is create mistrust or uncertainty in teachers that is eventually transmitted to students. An administrator's classroom visits balloon in significance, since they may have a direct effect on a teacher's livelihood. Furthermore, the tone of such an approach is incompatible with the spirit of support, encouragement, and progress described in New Testament literature.

Sample Purpose Statement

> Supervision will be aimed at improving teachers' skills, the instructional process, and learning outcomes. Because teachers are indwelt by God the Holy Spirit and are called to Christian school teaching, they can be trusted to press on toward improvement and maturity, both personal and professional. It is assumed that teachers' contracts will be renewed each year unless God moves them elsewhere or their performance indicates a misplacement in ministry.

Notice in this sample statement the assumption that teachers will be successful and that contracts *will* be renewed unless decisions are made otherwise. This assumption frees supervisors to concentrate on assisting teachers to improve their instructional skills. Though the time may come when it becomes obvious that certain teachers are not suited to continuing in their field, the main thrust of this policy is to keep teachers from reaching that point by enabling them to be increasingly successful.

Responsibilities for Supervision

Supervision policies should also describe, in general terms, the responsibilities of personnel in the supervisory process. These responsibilities should be stated broadly enough that reassignment of supervisory duties within administrative staffs will not require policy changes to keep up with new duties. Reshuffling specific supervisory functions may become necessary for several reasons: (1) schools may grow, adding administrators; (2) schools may become smaller, requiring consolidation of duties; (3) different approaches to supervision may be initiated, such as peer coaching or mentoring; or (4) supervisory duties may be reassigned to persons with specific abilities.

Thus it is advisable to describe the responsibilities in a way that gives administrators authority over the school's broad supervisory practices but leaves specific techniques and procedures to the administrators' discretion.

Sample Responsibilities Statement

Responsibility for supervision of teachers rests with administrators, who must exercise gentleness in an unpretentious manner. They are responsible for developing procedures that will help teachers improve the quality of their instruction. Teachers are accountable for personal evaluation, examination, and growth but are submissive to administrative supervision, making an administrator's work rewarding.

Nature of Supervisory Activities

This section of supervision policies provides general guidance for supervisory activities. For example, it may discuss:

1. Teacher self-evaluations
   Sample: *All teachers will conduct annual self-appraisals that they will share in conference with the administrator.*
2. Classroom observations
   Sample: *Classroom observations are considered essential in the process of helping teachers improve. Administrators will arrange for all teachers to be observed.*
3. Peer coaching or mentoring
   Sample: *At the discretion of the administrator, peer coaching or mentoring may be used as a tool for supervision and instructional improvement.*
4. Individual teacher improvement plans
   Sample: *All teachers will prepare annual improvement objectives that they will share in conference with the administrator.*
5. Videotaping
   Sample: *Videotaping of classroom activities is a valuable means of providing feedback for teachers. However, videotaping must be voluntary, and tapes of classes must remain the property of teachers.*
6. Sources of information about teacher performances other than direct observation by administrators
   Sample: *Administrators should develop careful guidelines for receiving data on teacher performance. The principles from Matthew 5 and 18 must be obeyed.*
7. Differentiated supervision
   Sample: *In recognition of the differences in teachers' knowledge and expertise, the supervision requirements for teachers will be flexible.*

It is not necessary to address all these topics in a given school's supervision policies. Some can be left to administrator discretion. Christian school boards, however, should be careful to give administrators sufficient policy guidance

(1) to protect administrators from single-handedly fielding too many potentially volatile issues (such as the dismissal of a teacher) and (2) to ensure stability and continuity in personnel matters during changes in the administrative staff. Boards must find the right balance in policies that are inclusive yet general. Details not included in the policy can be developed as components of the school's supervision plan.

Intensive Correction Period and Nonrenewal or Termination of Contract

As noted above, the primary purpose of supervision is to improve teachers' classroom instruction. This statement assumes that administrators and boards will recruit and hire teachers in whom they have confidence. Christian schools should hire teachers with the expectation that they will be successful, and they should avoid hiring those whose success appears questionable. If an administrator hires a teacher of whom he is not fully confident, he should intend that the teacher will get enough supervisory assistance to become successful.

Given such employment practices, teachers are able to start each school year with the security that contract renewal from year to year is the normal expectation. This is not to suggest that a formal tenure system should be established but that schools should operate according to the principle that love expects the best from people. Thus, teachers can expect to be retained. Annual votes to renew teacher contracts should be unnecessary or a mere formality.

1. **Intensive Correction Period**

   As much as administrators and boards want all teachers to be successful in the classroom, there are likely to be some who struggle so much that administrators lose confidence that they will ever succeed. It is only fair to inform such teachers of their deficiencies and tell them clearly that contract renewal is no longer automatic but is open to question. These teachers should be given a correction period (possibly three months) in which to rectify the problems. During this period, classroom observation serves two purposes: (1) to improve instruction, and (2) to serve as the basis for contract renewal or nonrenewal. At the conclusion of this period, one of the following decisions is made: (1) the teacher has rectified the deficiencies, and the contract will be renewed; (2) the teacher has not corrected the shortcomings and the contract will not be renewed; or (3) the teacher has not removed all deficiencies but has shown enough progress that the contract can be renewed under continued "intensive correction" status; further improvement is required, and future contract renewal is not yet assured.

2. **Nonrenewal**
    When a teacher's contract expires, there is no legal obligation to renew it or even to give a reason for its nonrenewal. A nine-month contract that expires on June 15 simply ceases to exist as a contract on June 16. However, Christian school administrators have moral obligations to be truthful and open with struggling teachers and to provide them with all possible assistance up to the contract closure date. It is incompatible with biblical principles to announce nonrenewal without having forewarned the teacher and provided an intensive correction period. (For more on the Intensive Correction Period, see chapter 15, "Working with the Marginal Teacher.")

3. **Termination**
    Another personnel action that occasionally surfaces is the termination of a contract. Termination is the cancellation of a contract before its expiration date. Policies on contract termination should include procedures for processing such decisions. For example, the policies should identify causes for which a teacher may be terminated, procedures for termination, and provisions for the teacher to follow in making an appeal. Reasons for contract termination should be stated in a school's standard teacher contract. Termination procedures should contain several ingredients to ensure fair and thorough processing of decisions, including:
    • Clear and timely notice of pending termination, along with reasons
    • Opportunity for the teacher to present contrary evidence
    • Opportunity for the teacher to be heard before the school board
    • Adherence to the stipulations of the school's constitution, bylaws, faculty handbook, and teacher contract[3]

Even though nonrenewal and termination are negative experiences, administrators can help the teachers involved to sense God's sovereignty in their lives. In doing so, administrators can emphasize those strengths and abilities that may equip them to serve more effectively in other areas of ministry. Ideally, teachers will come to view nonrenewal or termination not as failure and personal rejection but as God's way of leading them to another form of service.

Chapter Summary

Supervision policies in Christian schools are essential. They form the basis for instructional improvement practices and evaluation of teaching personnel. Their development should include input from board members, teachers, and administrators. Every supervision policy should address key issues including the purpose for supervision, the supervisor's responsibilities, the nature of supervisory activities, a description of intensive correction periods, and procedures for the nonrenewal of contracts.

Supervisor's Prayer

Dear Father in heaven, How grateful I am for the tender way that you consistently endure my weaknesses and blunderings, always seeking to shape me into the image of Christ. Grant me the ability, I pray, to show your love in this same way to my teachers. May I lead our school in the preparation of fair and righteous policies that reflect your mercy, as well as your concern for order and justice. May people experience your love and security as these policies are followed. I pray that our school will represent you well in its personnel matters in order that you may receive great honor and glory. For Jesus' sake, Amen.

Endnotes

1. Myron Rush, *Management: A Biblical Approach* (Wheaton, IL: Victor Books, 1984), 19–31.
2. Ronald T. Hyman, *School Administrator's Faculty Supervision Handbook* (Englewood Cliffs, NJ, 1986), 11–18.
3. Ibid., 25.

Materials on Disk

Form 01 Christian School Supervision Policy

3

The Role of the Teacher Job Description

But now God has placed the members, each one of them,
in the body, just as He desired.
(1 Corinthians 12:18)

Chapter highlights....

Purposes of job descriptions
Preparation of job descriptions
Format and style
Suggestions for use
Sample forms

J ob descriptions are dead documents in many schools. Originally created to meet accreditation requirements, they remain hidden in big binders on office shelves or tucked away in teacher manuals. They are rarely referenced.

Actually, job descriptions can and should serve pivotal functions in Christian school supervision. They should be living documents that guide all facets of faculty selection, performance, supervision, and evaluation.

Job descriptions are formal statements that outline the minimum qualifications, duties, responsibilities, channels of supervision and accountability, and essential functions for each position in an organization.[1] Most Christian schools prepare generic position descriptions that apply to groups of teachers, such as elementary and secondary, rather than a separate one for each grade level or academic discipline. Such generic descriptions set forth the qualifications and duties of all faculty members in the applicable groups. Some schools prepare individual job descriptions for each position, though this practice is infrequent.

A Biblical Basis Before we look at job descriptions in detail, we would do well to determine whether the use of this administrative tool is compatible with biblical views of people management. In other words, does Scripture support our use of job descriptions?

Although no Scripture addresses the question directly, there are numerous passages in which the specifying or listing of tasks, assignments, or general duties was done with God's blessing. First Corinthians 12, for instance, lists the functions of church members, and 1 Peter 5 describes the role of elders. Still other New Testament passages give specific instructions to certain persons for work they were to perform. Old Testament examples include Exodus 35–38, which specifies workers' tasks in building the tabernacle; Leviticus, which describes the work of priests in the sacrificial system; and Nehemiah, which defines the responsibilities of those rebuilding the Jerusalem wall. In general, it seems that God's principles for decency and order encourage the practice of specifying job responsibilities.

What Are the Purposes of Job Descriptions?

The role of job descriptions should be central in faculty selection, performance, supervision, and evaluation. They are equipped for these functions because they usually outline the minimum qualifications and the main responsibilities of teachers. They may also set forth standards for acceptable performance and procedures for evaluation. Thus job descriptions have three main purposes: (1) to guide faculty appointments, (2) to guide faculty performance, and (3) to guide faculty evaluation.

Guiding Faculty Appointments Job descriptions for teachers should clearly articulate the qualifications of persons hired for teaching positions. When they do so, they can be used to inform inquirers of what the school expects of teachers. If potential applicants see that they lack some requisites, they may eliminate themselves from consideration before they apply, conserving administrative processing time. According to Harris, "a job description should contain all of the essential information that a prospective employee would need in order to 'size up' the job."[2] The lists of qualifications may also help administrators and boards to focus on the essential qualities they desire in teachers.

The job description should describe (or reference another document that describes) the "essential functions" of each position in sufficient detail that applicants can determine whether their health or disability would require the school to make "reasonable accommodations." The Americans with

Disabilities Act (ADA) is the federal law that applies here. The school should be proactive in defining the "essential functions" of teaching. Otherwise, the Equal Employment Opportunities Commission (EEOC) may help to define those functions if a case is brought before it. For a more detailed discussion of the issue, see ACSI's *Personnel Forms Resource Packet*.[3]

Guiding Faculty Performance Job descriptions also serve as valuable guides for teachers as they minister, fulfill responsibilities, and complete tasks. To make descriptions valid for this purpose, they should not simply be borrowed from other schools, but should be forged from the perspectives and convictions of the schools using them. From these descriptions, teachers can set personal improvement goals, and administrators can be clear about what functions are, and are not, expected of teachers.

Guiding Faculty Evaluation By spelling out what schools expect of teachers, job descriptions can serve as bases for teacher supervision and evaluation. While they typically do not articulate details about teacher performance, they do codify categories of behavior that make up a teacher's total ministry in the school. Thus they can guide administrators in making a summative evaluation of each teacher's performance, and they can guide each teacher in preparing a self-evaluation.

How Are Job Descriptions Prepared?

The road to preparing job descriptions has some possible potholes, including the following: (1) they may be too general, lacking enough detail to be useful; (2) they may contain unrealistic expectations or idealistic standards that discourage teachers from making serious attempts to conform to them; and (3) they may be prepared by one administrator without the input of others and thus may lack the understanding and support of the teachers and other administrators.

Despite potential drawbacks, however, school staffs can create useful job descriptions that serve their intended purposes. As in developing a supervisory policy, it is good to involve both administrators and teachers.

Should job descriptions be borrowed? Certainly, it is wise to consult job descriptions that others have worked hard to produce. Sample job descriptions like the one in this chapter include most of the important features, and it is probably wise to reference those of other Christian schools in order to see the varied ways of constructing them. In addition, the Association of Christian Schools International (ACSI) has created a sample job description for teachers that is available in its *Personnel Forms Resource Packet*.[4] However, whatever examples are examined, a school's job descriptions should be tailored to the specific school and faculty.

Who should prepare job descriptions? Job descriptions are tools to assist in carrying out personnel policies. As such, they should be approved by those who are one level above the persons they govern. Thus administrators should approve teacher job descriptions, and the school board should approve those of administrators. However, it is also essential for those who must follow the descriptions to participate in developing them. As Ben Harris says, "Effective staff relationships will depend upon some substantial degree of clarity about job responsibilities and mutual acceptance thereof."[5]

What is a suggested procedure? Though there are numerous possible procedures for developing job descriptions, the following provides an efficient balance between faculty input and administrative leadership:

1. The administrator gathers sample descriptions and adds some personal ideas. (*Suggestion:* Consult the ACSI Christian school directory and request samples from both large and small schools in various regions of the country.)
2. Faculty suggestions are solicited and collected. (Either a brainstorming session or written questionnaire may be appropriate.)
3. A faculty committee reviews the samples, the administrator's ideas, and input from all teachers.
4. The faculty committee prepares a draft of the job description for administrative review.
5. The administrator edits the job description for completeness, alignment with the school's mission and policies, and proper format.
6. The administrator gives final approval to the job description.

What Style and Format Should Be Used?

Style Job descriptions should be easy to read and understand. Excess verbiage should be eliminated, and the style should be consistent. Lloyd Dull suggests the following guidelines:

1. Use a terse and direct style. *Example*: "Prepares and submits weekly lesson plans for administrator's review."
2. Keep sentence structure simple. *Example*: "Maintains a clean, attractive classroom."
3. Omit all words and phrases that do not contribute necessary information. Example: "Uses acceptable English in written and oral communication" rather than "Uses the kind of English that is commonly accepted in interpersonal and professional written and oral communication."

4. Begin each sentence with an action verb, third person singular. *Examples*: Develops, Makes, Exercises, Provides, Keeps.
5. Emphasize the skills and purposes of the job. *Example*: "Uses homework effectively for drill, review, enrichment, or project work" rather than "Uses good judgment in assigning homework."[6]

Format Job descriptions should contain several features, including:
1. Job title (*optional:* a paragraph containing a general description of the position)
2. Job's position in the chain of supervision (who supervises the teachers?)
3. Skills, knowledge, abilities, and convictions required
4. Major performance responsibilities of the job, detailed enough to be descriptive but general enough to cover omissions
5. May also include evaluative criteria for personnel performance reviews

How Can Job Descriptions Be Used?

Job descriptions provide guidelines for teachers to reference as they set annual goals for self-improvement, staff development, and professional advancement.[7] They may be used by both teachers and supervisors for a complete cycle of personnel supervision. Specific applications include:
1. *Setting self-improvement goals.* By using self-appraisal forms that correspond item by item to job descriptions, teachers can evaluate their past performances and set new improvement goals. (See forms on disk.)
2. *Teacher training.* It is often valuable to conduct faculty sessions on sections of their job descriptions. Such sessions usually provoke stimulating examination of schools' philosophies and purposes, as well as teachers' roles in fulfilling those goals.
3. *Teacher evaluation.* If teacher evaluation instruments used by administrators correspond item by item to job descriptions, they create coherence in the evaluation cycle which, in turn, produces valid evaluations.

A Word About the Sample Job Description

The sample form is applicable to Christian school teachers. It is meant to suggest a starting point for schools as they tailor teacher job descriptions to the particulars of their ministries. The job description included here was developed from a cross-section of Christian school documents by supervision students in one of the author's classes.

Suggested Plan for Use

1. The form is constructed so teachers can use it for personal evaluation and for the setting of improvement goals and plans. One application is for teachers to self-evaluate on all the items using the ranking categories on the form. These rankings could remain private to the teachers and need not be shown to administrators. However, the improvement goals that arise from the evaluations may be recorded on the companion form (also on the disk) and shared with administrators in start-of-the-year goal-setting conferences. Administrators can use these goals as a guide to praying for teachers during the year.
2. Administrators may also use the form for summative, end-of-year evaluations (see chapter 16).
3. The "Instructional" section of the job description may provide the basis for classroom observation and evaluation. This can be effected by replacing the ten general behaviors with numerous specific in-class behaviors that characterize good teaching (see chapter 7). In this way, an instrument is available for classroom observation that is consistent with the job description.

Summary

Teacher job descriptions provide the core around which faculty recruitment and appointment, performance, and evaluation revolve. Their use is supported biblically by examples of orderliness and the prescription of duties in the Scriptures. The best job descriptions incorporate insights of board members, administrators, and teachers. The format and style are terse and direct, without excess verbiage. Job descriptions can be used by teachers in self-evaluation and by administrators in summative evaluations at the end of the school year.

Supervisor's Prayer

Dear Lord, I worship you for being a God who has communicated clearly with humankind. Your standards and expectations are revealed for all to see. In the same way, grant me the ability to communicate clearly with my teachers and staff so that misunderstandings about job expectations do not arise. I desire that this school be conducted decently and in order. May your indwelling Spirit enlighten my way each day as I help subordinates understand and perform their ministries. Amen.

Endnotes

1. Lloyd Dull, *Supervision: School Leadership Handbook* (Columbus, OH: Charles E. Merrill Publishing Company, 1981), 96.
2. Ben Harris, et al., *Personnel Administration in Education* (Boston: Allyn and Bacon, 1979), 149.
3. Burt Carney, ed. *Christian School Personnel Forms* (Colorado Springs, CO: Association of Christian Schools, International, 2001), 3-1 to 3-3.
4. Ibid., 3-4 to 3-12.
5 Ben Harris, *Supervisory Behavior in Education* (Englewood Cliffs, NJ: Prentice-Hall, 1963), 137.
6. Dull, 96.
7. Keith A. Acheson and Meredith Gall, *Techniques in the Clinical Supervision of Teachers* (New York: Longman, 1997), 188.

Materials on Disk

Form 02 Christian School Teacher Job Description and Annual Evaluation
Form 03 Teacher Self-Improvement Goals

4

Planning for Differentiated Supervision

For which one of you, when he wants to build a tower, does not first sit down and calculate the cost, to see if he has enough to complete it?
(Luke 14:28)

Chapter highlights....

Guiding principles
Components of an annual plan
Introduction to differentiated supervision
Supervision levels
Process for classifying teachers
Differentiating intensity of supervision
Annual planning for supervision

Principal Johnson completed her round of classroom observations and follow-up conferences with her teachers. Though it was a demanding and draining task, she was committed to the importance of doing it each semester. This time, however, she deviated from her usual pattern of devoting a full week to the supervision of each teacher. Because of time pressures, she reduced the number of classroom observations for several teachers. These teachers were doing excellent work and direct observational supervision was not essential for them. Little did she expect the questions she would receive one day from two teachers to whom she had devoted the normal full week.

Miss Adams, a third-year teacher, inquired, "Mrs. Johnson, I'm not sure I understand why you felt it was necessary for you to visit my class three days when you observed several other teachers less often and, for one teacher, made no visits at all."

Mr. Stone, a twelve-year veteran, probed with, "Mrs. Johnson, please help me see why an experienced teacher like me was visited more often than a fifth-year teacher."

How was Principal Johnson to respond? It was clear to her that the differences in supervisory attention related to the quality and experience levels of the teachers. Shouldn't she have the administrative prerogative to treat teachers differently? Why did she sense that Miss Adams and Mr. Stone were subtly questioning her judgment, her motives, and her opinion of them as teachers? There must be a way to plan supervision that would ease the time pressures and would differentiate between teachers but would still retain their trust, she thought.

Simplistic solutions fail to meet these criteria. Each administrator faces variables that make generic solutions difficult to implement, or worse, irrelevant and ineffective. These variables may include:

- an administrator who teaches much of the day or one with no teaching assignment
- a mature teaching staff or a staff with many inexperienced teachers
- an administrator with educational expertise or one with minimal education training
- a teaching staff with a high turnover rate or a stable, long-term staff
- a board that is committed to staff development or one that emphasizes evaluation and summative judgments

Thus administrators must develop supervision plans that are appropriate for their particular contingencies. At the same time, all supervision plans should follow certain important principles, regardless of variables.

This chapter contains ideas for a month-by-month, teacher-by-teacher supervision plan. Its purpose is to give administrators a workable, yearlong structure for supervisory activities. Not every plan component is described in detail here because many are treated in greater depth in other chapters.

What Principles Should Guide Supervisory Plans?

Administrators should follow two broad principles when constructing a supervision plan:

1. *Biblical guidelines must be integrated into the "everydayness" of the plan's activities.* Biblical guidelines, discussed in chapter 1, direct the school's supervision activities most effectively when they translate from theory into practice. Thus, specific supervisory plans and procedures must reflect biblical principles. A good example is the manner in which administrators activate the Galatians 6:1 principle of restoring the one who falls. This

principle requires administrators to seek every means possible to assist struggling teachers. Does the supervision plan provide the floundering teacher with various kinds of assistance such as classroom observation, peer coaching, and professional training? Or does the teacher receive minimal help, and is she then left alone to self-correct?

2. *The school's supervision policy should govern the details of actual supervision activities.* Board members, administrators, and teachers must understand the relationship between stated policy and actual practice. Inconsistencies between the two lead to misunderstandings and confusion. For example, practice contradicts policy if policy states that the goal of supervision is to improve instruction, but the administrators prepare only summative renewal or dismissal judgments.

In addition to these two guidelines, several other principles are important:

Correct assumptions about Christian school teachers Supervisors should assume that teachers are motivated to improve their instruction and will respond to proper supervisory strategies. (See chapter 8 regarding teacher motivation.) Because of God's indwelling Holy Spirit, teachers see their work as a spiritual ministry and can be motivated on that basis. The supervision plan should reflect these assumptions.

An orderly, fair, workable plan Most administrators must schedule and plan supervision in order for it to happen. It will not take place if other urgent matters push it to the bottom of the priority list. Therefore, administrators should devise plans that are orderly, scheduled, and publicized appropriately to teachers. Faculty members must understand the process, its purposes, and their particular role.

Administrators should also prepare plans that are realistic. To meet the goals of supervision, they need to balance the ideal with the practical. For example, it may be ideal for the administrator to devote an entire week to each teacher, but that goal is unrealistic if the administrator teaches fifty percent of the day and directly supervises twelve teachers. A more workable plan may combine direct administrator involvement with indirect or alternative help for teachers. Administrators must be careful to schedule their supervision in such ways and at such times that other administrative demands do not supersede them.

Flexibility for meeting teachers' needs Not all teachers require the same degree of supervisory attention. Beginning teachers will need special assistance and guidance, but experienced, highly motivated teachers may be able to do some self-supervision or to assist in mentoring new teachers. Supervision plans should account for these differences. A plan for differentiated supervision is presented later in this chapter.

What Are the Components of an Annual Supervision Plan?

Yearlong supervision plans, whether differentiated or not, should contain three ingredients: (1) teacher evaluation and self-improvement goals, (2) a variety of supervision activities to help teachers reach their improvement goals, and (3) a year-end evaluation that summarizes teachers' total performance. The following chart shows the broad sweep of a yearly plan:

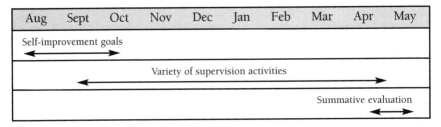

The supervisory year begins as teachers set self-improvement goals and share them with supervisors. It continues with the supervision of individual teachers through a variety of activities, including conferencing and classroom observation. Finally, it concludes with an annual evaluation. The following discussion looks at each phase in greater detail:

August–September

As mentioned, the plan begins as teachers set personal self-improvement goals for the coming school year. The goals for returning teachers should flow from their annual evaluation of the previous year. New teachers must construct goals from their knowledge of their strengths and weaknesses, perhaps gleaned from student teaching experiences.

Forms to use Two types of forms can assist teachers in preparing these goals. One type relates directly to the teacher job description (see chapter 3 and accompanying disk) and focuses on overall job performance expectations. Another type (on accompanying disk) should identify good instructional practices usually not mentioned in detail in the job description. The form or checklist that administrators use for classroom observation records is suitable for this purpose. By using both forms, teachers can self-evaluate and develop improvement goals in general job duties as well as specific instructional strategies.

Conferencing Teachers should share their improvement goals in conference with the appropriate administrator or supervisor. These conferences provide opportunity for collaboratively reviewing and refining goals, voicing encouragement and support for teachers, and praying for God's empowering and blessing. After the conference, both the teacher and administrator should retain copies of the goals. Throughout the year, wise administrators will make teachers' improvement goals the subject of regular prayer concern.

August–September checklist The following checklist serves as a reminder of August–September tasks related to goal-setting:

Administrator Tasks	Teacher Tasks
• Forms prepared and copied • Teacher conferences scheduled (Aug–Sept) • Conferences conducted • Improvement goals noted in personal prayer journal	• Self-evaluation forms completed on time • Conference held with supervisor • Plans for incorporating goals into daily activities

September–March

From September to March, administrators carry out supervision activities with individual teachers and with faculty groups. These activities may include classroom observation visits, conferences, peer supervision, videotaping, group in-service sessions, or other procedures. All these activities aim at each teacher's instructional improvement.

The key task for supervisors is to schedule classroom observations and teacher conferences. This task requires diligence and planning. Observation should be an integral part of the plan, not a rushed, last-minute afterthought. Thoughtful planning is required for administrators to implement systematic, quality supervision.

March

March is the traditional month for school boards to renew teacher contracts. In preparation, administrators should carefully prepare one of three recommendations for each teacher.

Renewal–unconditional The supervision policy described in chapter 2 assumes that administrators will recommend unconditional renewal for all teachers unless special conditions exist. This recommendation flows from the assumption that teachers will be successful and that supervision assists them in continuous improvement.

Nonrenewal A recommendation for nonrenewal of contract should be made only after the administrator has given the teacher a formal "intensive correction" period with clear notice that performance improvements are required for contract renewal. (For a detailed discussion of intensive correction, see chapter 15, "Working With the Marginal Teacher.")

Renewal–conditional A recommendation for conditional renewal should also be preceded by an intensive correction period for the teacher in question. In this case, the teacher may improve sufficiently so that future success seems likely but not certain. A conditional contract requiring continued improvement and intensive supervision in the next year may be appropriate.

May

In May, supervisors hold annual evaluation conferences with teachers. Though contract renewal time was probably in March or April, it was an automatic or assumed renewal for all teachers with the exception of those who are in intensive correction status or whose contract was not being renewed. Therefore, an annual summation of teachers' full-year performance would be incomplete if it was prepared in March. Since contract renewal is not in jeopardy, it is more beneficial to conduct annual evaluations closer to the end of the school year.

Annual evaluations give administrators opportunity to commend teachers for a job well done, to pray with them, and to help them chart their professional growth plans for the future. Teachers may use evaluations shared in these conferences as starting points for self-improvement goals for the next school year. The annual cycle may be pictured as:

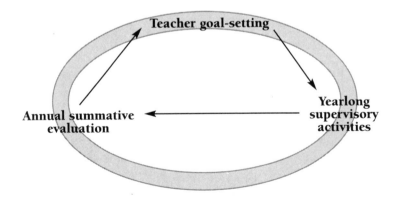

Introduction to Differentiated Supervision

Simply stated, differentiated supervision is an approach that provides teachers and supervisors with options about the kinds of supervisory and evaluative activities employed with each teacher.[1] This approach recognizes that teachers are at differing levels of personal and professional maturity, and thus require varying levels of supervision intensity.

Biblical principles This approach coincides well with the way God works with His children. Because Christians have different levels of spiritual maturity and different types of giftedness, God's plan for working in each believer's life is different. While God upholds and pursues His overall plan and goals, His activity may be quite different in one Christian's life than in another's. This principle suggests that Christian schools should consider permitting more individualized activities for supervising teachers.

Differences in teachers The fact that Christian school teachers are different was highlighted during a recent survey conducted among 800 Christian school administrators. Using three different managerial schemes for classifying subordinates, administrators selected six faculty members in their schools and applied each of the three classification templates to each teacher. The results? None of the 800 administrators reported that all six of their subordinates were classified identically on all three schemes, an overwhelming indication that differentiated supervision of Christian school teachers is a wise strategy that reflects reality.[2]

As an outgrowth of these principles and findings, this chapter describes a sample differentiated supervision plan. In order to avoid the appearance of inequity or favoritism on the part of the administrator, as Principal Johnson experienced, a formal plan or structure should be put in place. This plan should have the endorsement of the school's governing board, its administrators, and the faculty, and it should be built on five major goals:

Foundational Goals for a Differentiated Supervision Plan
- Follow a biblical model for dealing with persons as individuals.
- Provide supervision at level of each teacher's need.
- Provide opportunities and incentives for all teachers to grow in professional expertise.
- Make use of the knowledge and talents of experienced teachers.
- Decrease the administrator time required for direct classroom observation and conferencing.

What Levels of Supervision Intensity Are Appropriate?

The number of classifications of teachers may vary from school to school. Some public and Christian schools have two categories—tenured and non-tenured. A few schools have developed three levels for greater differentiation. Most colleges have at least four levels of faculty rank. The Cincinnati public schools have developed a five-tier system with levels called *apprentice, novice, career, advanced*, and *accomplished*.[3] The author suggests that schools classify teachers at three levels, for the following reasons:

• Four or more levels may be too cumbersome for most small or mid-sized schools. Some levels may remain unoccupied, with no teachers qualifying for them.

• Two levels are too restrictive of the distinctions that most schools will actually want to make. Usually schools will have teachers in three main tiers of experience, expertise, and quality of performance.

The three tiers of teacher classification should include all teachers from first-year to the seasoned. Logically, the three levels may be defined as:

Tier	Description
Beginning professional Apprentice First-level professional	The teacher is just starting and will benefit greatly from mentoring, or is experienced but struggling with teaching issues that beginning teachers usually overcome.
Intermediate professional Journeyman Second-level professional	The teacher has transitioned from needing mentoring to serving as a peer assistant to an equal. Has overcome new-teacher struggles and is becoming a proactive, contributing professional.
Resource professional Master Third-level professional	Teacher is recognized as a professional who can mentor others. Is capable of self-directed growth and development.

Several potential titles for the classification levels are suggested. Each school should decide what titles are suitable for it to use.

How Should Teachers Be Assigned to Different Tiers?

Tiering teachers, or classifying them, is key to a differentiated supervision plan. Instead of relying on an administrator's intuition, schools should employ a formal plan that classifies teachers by experience, quality of performance, intensity of supervision, and professional growth options.

Using a committee or board As one can imagine, the process for assigning teachers to the appropriate tiers could raise questions, especially if only one person is making the decisions. By investing a group (committee or board) with ultimate decision-making authority, schools employ the biblical principle that in the multitude of counselors there are wisdom and safety.

Qualification criteria for each level School personnel must exercise care in choosing the criteria that qualify teachers for each tier. Some combination of experience and quality should be used. Experience is easily quantifiable (in years) and is not open to subjective judgment, but quality is hard to measure objectively. Still, schools must try to recognize true teaching quality and make classification decisions that are free of prejudice or bias.

One way to determine quality can be the strength of the teachers' end-of-the-year evaluations. Ratings over several years can be quantified and used as evidence to support a teacher's promotion, or nonpromotion, to another level.

Another source of information on teaching quality may be a personal portfolio submitted by each teacher. The portfolio should contain documentation of the teacher's professional growth activities, examples of unit and lesson plans, videotapes of teaching, and reflective essays on how the person has developed as a teacher.

Sample criteria The following chart provides example of promotion criteria:

Level	Minimum Years Experience	Quality of Annual Evaluations	Other Supporting Evidence
Beginning professional	0	None available yet	Not applicable
Intermediate professional	4	Two most recent evaluations should rate above average quality	Portfolio of yearly plans, student work, teaching video, and list of professional development activities
Resource professional	9	Three most recent evaluations should rate high quality	Portfolio of yearly plans, student work, teaching video, list of professional development activities, and 15-page paper on personal philosophy of Christian education

First-time classification of teachers Two scenarios present unique questions for initially classifying teachers:

In one scenario, a school is implementing a tiered plan for the first time. The administration should consider beginning on a "time-delayed" basis. That is, several years (probably three) should elapse between the approval or adoption of the plan and its implementation. In other words, before administrators begin to classify teachers, they should have at least three summative evaluations, and the teachers should have been able to collect their portfolio contents.

In the other scenario, an experienced teacher joins the faculty. Now a judgment must be made about that teacher's initial classification. One suggestion is not to classify that teacher for the first year, giving her time to demonstrate a teaching quality equal or superior to the level she had reached at her previous school.

A process for promoting teachers As mentioned above, the school board or its designated subcommittee should make decisions about promotion. However, to ensure that the administrator is included, the following process for promotion is suggested:

Step	Issues to Be Determined	Responsibilities
One	Are minimum eligibility requirements met? • Years of experience? • Quality summative evaluations?	Teacher and immediate supervisor collaborate to determine whether minimum eligibility is satisfied.

If yes, proceed to step two.

Two	Are there sufficient portfolio artifacts to demonstrate quality teaching and contribution to school's mission?	Teacher and immediate supervisor evaluate whether portfolio is strong or needs additional materials.

If yes, proceed to step three.

Three	Teacher submits application for promotion to a team appointed by administrator.	Teacher submits application. Administrator appoints panel to review application and make a recommendation. Panel may include the administrator.

Four	Review panel evaluates promotion application and makes recommendation in favor of, or against, promotion.	Administrator and review panel prepare this recommendation.

If panel recommends yes, recommendation sent to school board or its designated subcommittee.

If panel recommends no, teacher is informed of the reasons and encouraged to work on professional development.

Five	School board makes determination on promotion.	School board or designated subcommittee.

If promotion is not approved, teacher is informed of the reasons and encouraged to work on professional development.

The teacher and immediate supervisor collaborate collegially at the start of this process. The promotion process should be a partnership endeavor, with the professional development of the teacher as a central goal.

The administrator will be involved in one of two ways. One way is to serve as a member of the review panel, which the administrator appoints, ensuring his input and agreement. A second way is for the administrator to delegate the promotion recommendation fully to the review panel and to accept its recommendation as his own. Wherever possible, the administrator should avoid making solitary decisions, especially if a school board is available to lend additional wisdom and authority.

How Does Supervision Differ from Level to Level?

The plan for differentiated supervision should describe the type of supervision from which teachers in each tier will benefit. Doing so permits dealing with teachers as individuals, saving the administrator time, employing the expertise of veteran teachers, and providing incentives for professional development to teachers at all levels.

Beginning professional (see also chapter 12) The beginning professional should receive direct, intensive supervision as a support mechanism to ensure success as an educator. These supervisory activities may include:

• Mentoring by a veteran teacher
• Two cycles of three classroom visits and conferences with a supervisor, one each semester (see chapter 12 for description of this method)
• Occasional "one-hour" interventions by supervisor or mentor as needed (described in chapter 5)

Intermediate professional (see also chapter 13) By contrast, the intermediate professional requires only moderately intensive supervision. This teacher has demonstrated a growing level of teaching excellence and is occasionally able to initiate self-evaluation and make recommendations for her own improvement. The supervisory activities for this teacher may include:

• Peer coaching with another equally ranked teacher
• One cycle per year of two to three classroom visits and conferences with a supervisor
• "One-hour" interventions by peer or supervisor as needed

Resource professional (see also chapter 14) The resource professional may require no formal observations. This person is a proven professional who has the expertise and initiative to self-correct. As a result, supervisory activities for this teacher may include:

• Peer coaching with another equally ranked teacher
• "One-hour" interventions by peer or supervisor as needed
• Personal setting of improvement goals, monitoring of progress, and conferencing with supervisor twice a year to report status of professional growth

Summarizing a Differentiated Supervision Plan

A chart summarizing a sample differentiated supervision plan of three tiers is on the CD-ROM disk accompanying this book.

Two cautions The differentiated supervision structure described above is intended to be only a sample. Administrators who want to develop a differentiated plan should customize it for their own school. In addition, such a plan should be built on the input and involvement of teachers, administrators, and school board members. A differentiated supervision plan can be threatening to some teachers, so great care and patience should be exercised.

An alternative In schools where (1) the administrator has adequate time for full supervision of each teacher's instruction, or (2) there are fewer than ten faculty members, or (3) the board, administration, and faculty prefer a uniform (nondifferentiated) plan, the alternative is a one-size-fits-all strategy. This approach has its merits and certainly has been the predominant scheme in schools for many years. Schools using this strategy should analyze it carefully to decide whether it fosters continuous teacher growth and development, improved teaching and learning, and efficient use of the administrator's time.

How Does One Put a Differentiated Supervision Plan into Practice?

Codify teacher characteristics Good supervision does not happen automatically. Administrators who want their schools to employ effective supervision are proactive in planning supervision strategies and activities for the year. They "get to their calendars before someone else does" to ensure that they give supervision its proper priority. A starting point for developing an annual plan is to focus on each teacher and his supervisory "quotient," which includes:

- the teacher's tier or level
- the amount of classroom observation and conferencing needed
- the person who should conduct the observation and conferencing
- the teacher's ability to serve as a peer mentor or coach, or as a part-time supervisor

The following form is a *sample guide* for codifying faculty characteristics:

Teacher	Grade	Tier	Supervision Required	Notes
Janet Williams	1	Resource professional	No formal visits Self-directed goals with reports to administrator once a semester	Mentor for Carol Smith
Carol Smith	1	Beginning professional	One-week cycle (fall and spring)	Mentored by Janet Williams
James Black	2	Intermediate professional	One-week cycle (fall)	Peer coach for Susan Stanford
Susan Stanford	2	Intermediate professional	One-week cycle (spring)	Peer coach for James Black
Barb Wilson	3	Resource professional	No formal visits Self-directed goals with reports to administrator once a semester	Serve as part-time primary supervisor Mentor for Linda Green
Linda Green	3	Beginning professional	One-week cycle (fall and spring)	Mentored by Barb Wilson

Apportion supervisory tasks Using the above chart, the school's administrator can identify the supervisory activities that she must conduct personally and those that she can delegate. For example, the administrator decides that, of the teachers requiring formal one-week visit cycles, she will personally supervise Carol Smith and Linda Green, the Beginning Professionals. She will also conference with the two Resource Professionals, Janet Williams and Barb Wilson, regarding progress on their self-directed improvement goals. In addition, she will be available for occasional "one-hour" special help sessions. Other formal observation and conferencing cycles will be assigned to the part-time primary supervisor. The goal is to ensure that quality supervisory attention is given to teachers at their level of need, an objective that can be accomplished in ways that do not demand the direct time and attention of the lead administrator.

Reserve supervisory time Once the administrator has established her supervisory workload, she then *blocks calendar time*, setting apart weeks for her formal classroom observations and for conferencing with the beginning professionals, as well as weeks for conferencing with the resource professionals. The administrator considers the blocked time for supervision as "untouchable," except for major safety emergencies requiring immediate, on-the-spot attention, but such emergencies are infrequent. All other persons or activities clamoring for the administrator's attention can wait 20 to 45 minutes until the administrator completes the classroom visit or teacher conference. (Chapter 5, "The Classroom Visit and Conferencing Cycle," discusses in greater detail the "one-week" and "one-hour" plans mentioned above.)

Chapter Summary

Using important biblical principles as a foundation, administrators should develop annual plans for supervisory activities that include initial goal-setting by teachers, year-long supervision of instruction, and year-end summative evaluations.

A viable strategy is to differentiate the intensity and type of supervision given to teachers according to their experience and quality of performance. Three tiers, or levels, of teachers offer workable classifications for identifying teachers as beginning, intermediate, and resource professionals. Careful processes for promoting teachers include utilizing the wisdom of several persons or groups, thus freeing the administrator from having to make solitary decisions that some may view as entirely subjective.

Once a school has developed and adopted a differentiated supervision plan, the administrator's tasks are to (1) analyze the supervision needs of teachers, (2) determine what tasks he must perform personally and what ones he can delegate, and (3) allocate priority time each semester for the needed supervision activities.

Supervisor's Prayer

Dear Heavenly Father, I thank you for the special privilege of shepherding this group of teachers. I recognize the importance of the responsibility that you have given me for the teachers' professional growth. With humility and submission, I fervently ask for your enabling to perform this task in your power. Grant me efficiency of time and schedule as well as wisdom and insight. The potential for eternal significance in our Christian school ministry is great, and I praise you in advance for the wonderful work you are going to perform in and through our teachers this year. Through Christ, my Savior, I pray, Amen.

Endnotes

1. Allan A. Glatthorn, *Differentiated Supervision* (Alexandria, VA: Association for Supervision and Curriculum Development, 1997), 3.
2. From Supervision of Instruction, an ACSI-sponsored seminar conducted by Gordon Brown in spring 2000.
3. Julie Blair, "Cincinnati Teachers to Be Paid on Performance," *Education Week* 27 (September 2000), 1.

Materials on Disk

Form 02 Christian School Teacher Job Description and Annual Evaluation
Form 03 Teacher Self-Improvement Goals
Form 04 Plan for Differentiated Supervision
Form 05 Summative Teacher Evaluation

5

The Classroom Visit and Conferencing Cycle

Finally, brethren, rejoice, be made complete,
be comforted, be like-minded, live in peace.
(2 Corinthians 13:11)

Chapter highlights....

Biblical principles
Clinical supervision cycle
Weekly supervision structure
One-hour interventions

What Biblical Principles Can Guide Classroom Visits and Conferencing?

Chapter 1 has presented biblical principles for organizational functioning as they apply to Christian school leadership. Several of the same principles apply to how administrators handle classroom visits and conferencing. By employing them, administrators align themselves with God's truth for relationships among believers, leading to productive supervision and satisfying relationships with teachers.

Principles from Biblical Guidelines

Principles	Comments
Teachers are intrinsically motivated to improve their teaching skills.	This assumption arises from the truth that God the Holy Spirit indwells Christian teachers. Therefore, supervisors should use an approach that gives teachers opportunities to suggest solutions and improvement plans.
The supervision process aims at helping teachers to improve.	Because teachers are intrinsically motivated to improve, supervisors do not need to conduct observations for inspection and judgment. The purpose of observation and conferencing is to assist teachers in their development as Christian educators.

Principles	Comments
Clear, honest communication between supervisor and teacher is necessary.	This principle calls for supervision practices that allow open discussion between administrator and teacher before and after the classroom observation. The administrator must be clear and honest in discussing the teacher's classroom performance so the teacher can make real improvement based on open truth, not truth that is partially concealed.
The administrator and teacher should approach supervision with mutual submission and humility.	Neither the supervisor nor the teacher is omniscient in educational matters. Each can learn from the other, but only if both contribute to the analysis of data and the setting of improvement plans.
Supervision should deal with verifiable truth, not rumor.	Objective information on classroom events is the foundation for making changes that will result in real improvement. Rumor can provide false impressions; decisions based on rumor are unlikely to effect constructive change in teacher performance.

Conference ⇒ observation ⇒ conference These biblical principles argue strongly for a supervision cycle in which supervisor and teacher confer both before and after the classroom observation. Communication before the visit enhances trust, clarifies lesson objectives and plans, and identifies areas in which the teacher wants or needs help. Visiting the classroom enables the administrator to collect firsthand data about teaching and learning activities. Conferencing afterward gives the teacher clear feedback, allows the teacher to suggest analyses and improvement plans, and strengthens the trust between teacher and administrator. This cycle is commonly called "clinical supervision."

What Is Clinical Supervision?

Although the sequence of a "pre-teaching conference," a "classroom visit," and a "follow-up conference" was suggested as early as 1925, it wasn't until the mid-1950s that Morris Cogan of Harvard University invented "clinical supervision," which was augmented by Robert Goldhammer, one of Cogan's graduate students.[1] The term "clinical" describes the up-close, diagnostic, one-to-one nature of the plan.[2] Through a cycle of steps including pre-conferencing, classroom observation and analysis, and post-conferencing, supervisors work with teachers to evaluate data and prepare improvement strategies. In recent years, clinical supervision has become a popular approach for involving teachers and administrators in nonjudgmental, collegial support for teacher improvement. Many Christian school administrators have adopted clinical supervision as their mode of operation.

Clinical supervision provides an action plan, or cycle, within which biblical principles can be practiced. Though not prescribed in Scripture, the cycle's steps are conducive to the outworking of biblical supervision principles described above. Administrators can feel comfortable that the cycle suggested by Cogan and updated by Goldhammer in 1980 promotes a supervisory policy that is consistent with Christian goals.[3]

A typical clinical supervision cycle Depending on whose version one encounters, clinical supervision cycles have a minimum of three steps and a maximum of eight. For most administrators, four steps should suffice:

Stage	Description
Pre-observation conference	This conference establishes rapport between supervisor and teacher, putting the teacher at ease regarding the purposes of the visit. The teacher helps the supervisor understand the students in the class to be visited and provides information on the lesson(s) to be observed. Teacher and supervisor agree on the major areas to be observed. (For a detailed discussion on conferencing, see chapter 10.)
Classroom observation(s)	During classroom visits, the supervisor records data on areas of concern. The goal is to collect as much objective information as possible and make subjective interpretations later. (For a detailed discussion of classroom observations, see chapter 11.)
Analysis and strategy	After the classroom visit, the supervisor reviews observation notes for teaching patterns, critical incidents, or recurring verbal and nonverbal behavior while deciding how to handle the teacher conference. The supervisor may ask (and answer) such questions as, Are my data assembled logically? What questions will I ask the teacher to provoke self-analysis? How likely is it that the teacher or supervisor will have to generate ideas?
Post-observation or supervisory conference	In this conference, the supervisor gives the teacher specific feedback on what was observed, encourages and assists the teacher in forming improvement plans, and arranges for follow-up.

How Should the Clinical Supervision Cycle Be Used?

Focus on one teacher per week Beginning in mid-September and continuing through early December, administrators should give their attention to supervising one teacher each week. In that week, administrators can use an activity cycle that permits in-depth, up-close (clinical) supervision. By devoting one week to each teacher who needs direct attention, the supervisor is more likely to provide meaningful assistance. The suggested cycle for one-teacher-per-week includes four stages:

Monday: pre-observation conference	The administrator and teacher meet to discuss the classes to be observed. The teacher shares lesson plans with administrator. Together, they decide the areas of instruction on which the observer will gather data. Prayer is offered. (See chapter 10.)
Tuesday–Thursday: classroom observations	The supervisor conducts successive visits for three days in the same class period. In addition to agreed-upon observation areas, the supervisor notes overall class climate, flow of instruction from day to day, how the previous day's homework is treated, and other variables not always seen in one-day visits. The supervisor videotapes the Wednesday session for later viewing with the teacher. (See chapter 11.)
Thursday: analysis and strategy	The administrator privately reviews observation data and determines questions and strategy for the conference.
Friday: post-observation conference	The administrator and teacher review data collected during the observations, including excerpts from the videotape. They discuss the significance of the data and formulate improvement plans.

Why multiple visits? Using successive, same-subject visits to a teacher's classroom has several advantages. First, both students and teacher become more accustomed to the supervisor's presence, increasing the possibility that the supervisor will observe natural classroom dynamics. Second, the supervisor learns more about the classroom and thus can help the teacher more. Finally, supervisors can observe the flow from one day to the next in a selected subject area. For example, they can note what teachers do with assignments given the day before. For all these reasons, more observations are more helpful than fewer.

Priority scheduling By following a one-teacher-per-week plan, administrators give quality attention to each teacher. However, to use such a format, they must do some advance planning. The following memo to faculty illustrates the time-blocking required to make supervision work.

TO: All Teachers
FROM: Headmaster David Williams
RE: Supervision Schedule

As we have discussed, I will be devoting one week to assisting each of you with instructional improvement goals. I approach this task with humility and prayerful concern. To make efficient use of time, I will follow the schedule printed below. Please be sure to have a chair located inconspicuously in the room for my use. Thank you.

Teacher	Monday: Pre-Observation Conference	Tuesday–Thursday: Observations	Friday: Post-Observation Conference
Jones	Sept 3, 10:30	Math, 9:30–10:15	Sept 7, 3:15
Smith	Sept 10, 3:15	TBA	Sept 14, 3:15
Wilson	Sept 17, 7:30	TBA	Sept 21, 12:30
Johnson	Sept 24, 3:15	TBA	Sept 28, 3:15

As this memo shows, Headmaster Williams knows the teachers' schedules in advance so that he can reserve conference times. Since he also knows that Miss Jones wants help with mathematics instruction, he can schedule a specific time for his classroom visits. For the other teachers, an exact time for classroom observations would be determined during the pre-observation conference.

Supervisor-teacher ratio   In order for a one-teacher-per-week supervision plan to work, each administrator or supervisor should be responsible for observing the classes of no more than twelve teachers. Even this is a major assignment. A ratio of one to seven would be ideal. For each teacher to receive equal supervisory attention, the supervisor-to-teacher ratio should permit a one-week cycle for each teacher in fall and another in spring.

Some administrators have direct responsibility for more teachers than the above format allows. How can they provide in-depth, individualized supervision? The first suggestion is to develop a differentiated supervision plan like the one described in chapter four. Such a plan makes quality supervision possible in two ways: reducing the number of teachers who need intense personal supervision and involving other personnel in the supervisory process. In a differentiated plan, administrators use several ways to secure assistance with supervision:

- **Allow master teachers to supervise themselves.** Master teachers do not require the concentrated supervisory attention that others do. On their own, they can draw up personal improvement goals, analyze videotapes of their classes, solicit appropriate student and parent feedback, research new and creative teaching ideas, and integrate improvements into their planning and teaching. They should, however, maintain accountability by reporting to and conferencing with supervisors concerning their progress (see chapter 14).

- **Use master teachers to supervise inexperienced teachers.** Administrators can delegate some supervisory responsibilities by coordinating schedules to enable master teachers to visit classes of inexperienced teachers. Administrators should maintain accountability by requiring master teachers to report to them on the progress of the teachers they supervise.

- **Use grade-level leaders or department heads as supervisors.** Schools with several sections of each grade, or several teachers in each department, usually assign some administrative time and responsibility to a senior teacher for supervision of these units. Teachers serving in these leadership roles can assist the school's head administrator by conducting observations for teachers in their departments. To make this possible, those teachers should have at least one free period each day for supervision.

Emphasis on continuous supervision and feedback. The supervision cycle presented here will tell administrators what they need to know about teacher performance and will give teachers regular improvement suggestions. Administrators who stay abreast of teacher performance can assess it quickly and accurately. They know when they have lost confidence in a teacher to the point that contract renewal is in jeopardy. They should be forthright with the teacher about substandard performance and place the teacher on "intensive correction" status.

How Can a "One-Hour" Plan Provide Assistance?

Laurie Harris, a southern California educator, describes a special plan that can be conveniently contained within a 60-minute period.[4] The plan is designed to assist teachers on short notice in a limited time. It can be initiated by a teacher who wants help with a besetting problem or an administrator who is aware that a certain teacher is struggling. The hour is divided into three 20-minute segments: a classroom observation, analysis of the observation, and a follow-up conference with the teacher.

Classroom visit (20 minutes) Because the one-hour plan focuses on teacher presentation skills, the supervisor/observer aims to record the teacher's words and actions in the clearest possible way. The observer must write fast and use recording shortcuts.

Analysis and preparation for the conference (20 minutes) The observer prepares to meet with the teacher, working in undisturbed, distraction-free isolation while reviewing the observation notes and comparing the teacher's behaviors with good teaching practices. The observer notes several commendable aspects of the teacher's work and identifies one area for improvement, perhaps the one for which the teacher requested the observation visit.

Follow-up conference (20 minutes) Twenty minutes after the visit's conclusion, the teacher and observer meet for a follow-up conference. The observer establishes a friendly, supportive tone, remembering that the observation is formative and developmental, not judgmental and evaluative. She makes positive comments about the teacher's performance before moving into an area for improvement. In some cases, "coaching" or reteaching an important teaching skill may be appropriate. Finally, she concludes with prayer.

This one-hour intervention can be used as often as needed. For some teachers, numerous uses would be welcome; for others, no observation is necessary. The plan always aims at helping the teacher develop better instructional skills.

Chapter Summary

This chapter describes a teacher assistance cycle that includes a conference, classroom visits, analysis of the data, and a follow-up conference. This cycle, called "clinical supervision," activates important biblical principles for working with teachers. Administrators are encouraged to visit teachers' classes on three successive days in order to see natural classroom dynamics and to collect more information and thus be more helpful. To ensure that administrators give adequate attention to observing and conferencing, they need to reserve the time in advance, and they must not allow other matters to interfere. Administrators may also use a one-hour plan that provides "as needed" assistance to teachers.

Supervisor's Prayer

Dear Heavenly Father, I thank you for the special privilege of shepherding this group of teachers. I recognize the responsibility you have given me for their professional growth. With humility and submission, I ask for your enabling to perform this task in your power. Grant me efficient use of time as well as wisdom and insight. The potential for eternal significance in our Christian school ministry is great, and I praise you for the wonderful work you are doing through our teachers this year. Through Christ, my Savior, Amen.

Endnotes

1. Edward Pajak, *Approaches to Clinical Supervision: Alternatives for Improving Instruction* (Norwood, MA: Christopher-Gordon Publishers, 2000), 4–5.
2. Morris L. Cogan, *Clinical Supervision* (Boston: Houghton Mifflin, 1973).
3. Robert Goldhammer, Robert H. Anderson, and Robert J. Krajewski, *Clinical Supervision.* 2d ed. (New York: Holt, Rinehart, Winston, 1980).
4. Laurie Harris, "Teacher Evaluations: How to Observe and Conference for Results" (Tape 1). Produced for the International Fellowship of Christian School Administrators, 1998.

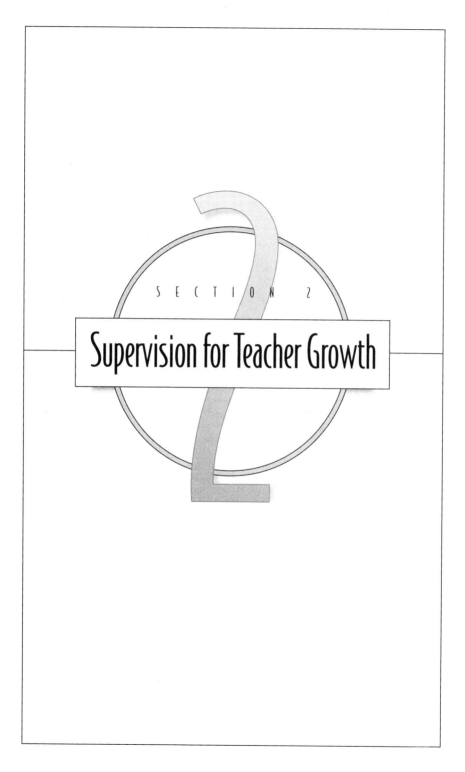

SECTION 2

Supervision for Teacher Growth

6

The Effective Supervisor

*I press on toward the goal for the prize of the
upward call of God in Christ Jesus.*
(Philippians 3:14)

Chapter highlights....

Leadership and a walk with God
Qualifications for spiritual leadership
Qualifications for educational leadership
Enhancing supervisory skills
The same person as supervisor and evaluator

"**M**rs. Williams, how will you know when you have become a good supervisor?" the interviewer asked.

"I suppose," Mrs. Williams responded, "when my teachers have all become good teachers."

"But can't you be a good supervisor before that?"

"Yes. No doubt I will have been a good supervisor for some time if my teachers eventually become good teachers."

"But if you have to wait for the results to know whether you are doing things right, how can you be sure you aren't experimenting aimlessly with your supervisory practices?"

Mrs. Williams furrowed her brow and responded slowly: "Because I don't have to reinvent the wheel: I only have to make it roll down my street."

As Mrs. Williams implies, we already know the characteristics of good supervisors and the ingredients of successful supervision. The proven elements of success spring from biblical principles, the experiences of others, and research findings. Utilizing them—making them roll down our street—makes our success as supervisors highly probable. The challenge is to acquire the skills and to apply them to our particular school situation. This chapter describes the qualities and skills of good supervisors. Having received a clear call from God to Christian school leadership, an administrator who relies on the Holy Spirit's gifting can develop the necessary skills and knowledge.

How Does a Walk with God Relate to Leadership?

The most important qualifications of Christian school supervisors result from a close relationship with God. This is true for two reasons:

First, the character qualities of God Himself are the ultimate purposes for pursuing God-honoring instructional practices in Christian schools. When God's character is formed in administrators, the schools they lead are energized by eternal purposes, and purpose is the greatest quality of leadership. Without purpose, leadership and supervision become passionless, self-serving, and lacking in direction. Administrators unlock the gate of God's purposes when they live in daily submission to their Heavenly Father.

Second, schools become the shadows of their administrators. Just as students who are fully taught will be like their teachers (Luke 6:40), so Christian schools will reflect the strengths and limitations of their administrators. Unless administrators are prepared to lead by example, they should not expect spiritual and academic excellence from teachers and students.

Several years ago, a Christian high school conducted a spiritual emphasis week. The administrator attended the meetings each day, praying that God would do a reviving work in students' hearts, but by midweek, he realized he'd been praying the wrong prayer. "Father, revive me," he asked, concluding that he could not expect something from faculty and students when he was not experiencing it himself. God spoke to his heart and gave him a revived commitment to holiness. The next day the special speaker was unexpectedly called out of town and could not conduct the closing meeting. The administrator, filled with fresh eternal purpose, delivered the chapel message as a stand-in. That day God used the words from the administrator's personal revival to stir the hearts of many students.

In this case, the administrator's shadow had begun to fall across the school. The values close to his heart were making their way into the climate of the school. But the shadow can also be negative when good values are far from an administrator's heart and therefore have little emphasis or visibility before staff and students.

What Are the Qualifications for Spiritual Leadership?

A walk with God is the foundation on which we can erect the qualifications for spiritual leadership. The New Testament identifies the qualities required in church leaders who oversee others in spiritual matters. Since leading Christian school teachers to instructional excellence is both a spiritual and a professional ministry, supervisors should have some of the same qualities that are expected of church leaders. These leadership qualities, as listed by Timothy and Titus, form three major categories:

1. **Personal qualities that make administrators worthy of imitation** A spiritual leader should be (1) above reproach, (2) hospitable, (3) a lover of the good, (4) devout, (5) one who holds fast the Word, (6) temperate, and (7) well thought of by outsiders. In other words, administrators who attend first to their personal spiritual well-being develop a base of respect from which to launch successful relationships and leadership.

2. **Interaction qualities that enable supervisors to conduct harmonious relationships with superiors, peers, and subordinates.** Thus, spiritual leaders are (1) not self-willed, (2) not quick-tempered, (3) not pugnacious, (4) gentle, and (5) self-controlled. In general, spiritual leaders are to be calm in spirit and to demonstrate genuine concern for others. Administrators who get upset, moody, or combative will not enjoy consistently productive interactions with teachers.

3. **Organizational qualities that equip administrators to lead, guide, and motivate others** Spiritual leaders are to be (1) sensible, (2) just, (3) able to teach, (4) able to manage, and (5) not novices. When administrators are mature, teachers are more likely to respond positively to supervision.

Should persons who are deficient in these biblical qualities be supervisors in Christian schools? Certainly God can take fledgling leaders and use them for His glory. But it is more in keeping with His sense of order to appoint supervisors who have the qualifications listed in Timothy and Titus. God gave us these instructions for good reason, and those charged with selecting administrators are wise not to circumvent His standards. Placing unqualified persons in administrative positions is a disservice to them and to those they lead.

What Are the Qualifications for Educational Leadership?

Once the spiritual qualifications are in place, we may look for the personal and professional qualities needed for educational leadership. These have been listed in various ways, and although each listing is unique, similarities exist. To set the stage, here are several inventories of supervisory qualities:

Modern Studies

Blome study In 1980, Dr. Blome of Western Kentucky University conducted a survey in which teachers highlighted what they saw as the traits of good supervisors. Their list includes:
(1) Leadership, confidence, willingness to help
(2) Ability to set a constructive, helpful climate
(3) Cooperative attitude
(4) Empathy with teachers and children
(5) Sincere interest in people and education[1]

Fortosis survey In 1982, Anthony Fortosis of ACSI replicated Blome's study with Christian school teachers. His survey includes:
(1) Spiritual qualifications
(2) Enthusiasm
(3) Concern for interpersonal relations
(4) Experience in education
(5) Availability to give help

Teachers in the Christian school survey also identified the type of help they expected supervisors to give. Their expectations were:
(1) Assistance with teaching methods
(2) Individual help from a professional
(3) Observations followed by conferences
(4) Frequent informal conferences[2]

Blumberg and Greenfield study In 1980, Arthur Blumberg and William Greenfield analyzed eight case studies to isolate the characteristics of effective instructional leaders. Among them are:
(1) An ability to set clear goals and use them in motivating subordinates
(2) A high degree of self-confidence and openness to others
(3) Tolerance for ambiguity
(4) Sensitivity to the dynamics of power
(5) An analytic perspective[3]

Gersten and Carnine analysis An analysis conducted in 1981 by Russell Gersten and Douglas Carnine identified several supervisory functions of good administrators:

(1) Implementation of programs known for instructional effectiveness
(2) Monitoring of student performance
(3) Monitoring of teacher performance
(4) Concrete technical assistance for teachers
(5) Visible personal commitment to programs for instructional improvement
(6) Emotional support and incentives for teachers[4]

Sheppard's findings In 1996, Sheppard synthesized the research on instructional leadership behaviors. He confirmed that principal behaviors relating to teachers' performance were:

(1) Framing and communicating school goals
(2) Supervising and evaluating instruction
(3) Coordinating the curriculum
(4) Monitoring student progress
(5) Protecting instructional time
(6) Maintaining high visibility
(7) Providing incentives for teachers
(8) Promoting professional development
(9) Providing incentives for learning[5]

Other studies Miscellaneous studies in past years have indicated other qualities, including:

(1) Intelligence
(2) Successful teaching experience
(3) Ability to speak and write fluently
(4) Skill in group dynamics
(5) Understanding of the learning process
(6) Ability to conduct and evaluate research
(7) Adeptness in decision-making

Synthesis of Key Qualities

From these studies emerges a description of good supervisors. The description has three categories—personal, relational, and managerial.

Good supervisors have exemplary personal qualities. They are:
- Spiritually qualified
- Enthusiastic about God's work and their calling
- Confident
- Tolerant of ambiguity, functioning in an orderly manner in the midst of uncertainty
- Committed to excellence

Good supervisors can work successfully with others. They are:
- Available, recognizing the immediacy of many needs
- Concerned for harmonious relationships
- Approachable, open, and honest with teachers
- Sensitive to the proper use and the misuse of their authority
- Able to conduct conferences in an atmosphere of trust
- Able to set and use goals to motivate themselves and others
- Able to provide emotional support for teachers
- Able to provide incentives for teachers
- Able to communicate their meaning clearly
- Understanding of the dynamics of group relationships
- Qualified to promote professional development

Good supervisors have management skills and educational expertise. They can:
- Supervise and evaluate instruction
- Implement programs that lead to instructional effectiveness
- Coordinate the curriculum
- Monitor teacher performance in mutually acceptable ways
- Monitor student progress
- Arrive at good decisions
- Share personal experience in education
- Describe, model, and implement teaching methods
- Offer concrete technical assistance
- Understand child development and learning processes
- Conduct and evaluate research

Not surprisingly, the qualifications for spiritual leadership (personal, interactive, and organizational) parallel those for educational leadership. This is as it should be, for in Christian school administration, leadership is both a professional and a spiritual ministry.

How Can Supervisory Skills Be Developed?

Good supervisors are made, not born. Through practice and training, inexperienced administrators can develop the qualities and improve the skills they need to lead their schools to excellence. Two prerequisites to growth and improvement are as follows:

• **A personal walk with God** The spiritual condition of administrators affects every aspect of supervision. No amount of training in supervision methods can make up for a listless devotional life. The vibrancy, love, and purpose needed to succeed as a Christian school administrator is God-breathed.

• **The conviction that God has called one to this ministry** With this conviction, administrators see purpose in their work, and they pursue excellence aggressively. Lacking the call of God, one may be misplaced in a supervisory position. When a school becomes stagnant, all too often it is because the administrators are not spiritually, personally, or professionally suited for leading teachers and students. Christian school administrators must have a Spirit-given certainty that God has placed them in their ministry.

Skills Development

On a foundation of spiritual vitality, administrators must build the skills and knowledge they need for proper supervision. What administrator does not expect teachers to know their subjects well and to teach them with precision and depth? In the same manner, administrators should be skilled in supervisory practices and knowledgeable in educational theory. Administrators with only a general and superficial understanding of teaching and supervision cannot give teachers the precise, insightful leadership they need to develop instructional excellence. Just as no amount of training in supervision can substitute for a listless spiritual life, so no amount of spiritual depth can take the place of professional expertise.

What can administrators do to improve in their supervisory roles? First, *they can take a personal inventory* to discover how well they are equipped for successful supervision in terms of the qualities and skills described above. Perhaps faculty input plus personal analysis can provide the answers needed.

Second, *they can determine the areas in which they need most improvement.* Third, *they can develop and initiate action plans designed to bring about growth in those areas.* The following suggestions are offered as ways to work toward becoming a better supervisor. Perhaps they can serve as starting points, provoking the reader's creativity to add others.

To develop good relations with subordinates	Practice listening. Have an "open door" office policy. Demonstrate trustworthiness. Be empathetic to teachers' needs.

To improve conferencing skills	Read a good counseling book. Practice conferencing with friends. Ask teachers for feedback on current conferencing skills. Videotape conferences for personal analysis. Discuss conferencing methods with pastors or local counselors.

To improve classroom observation skills	Visit classes using a variety of observation instruments. Videotape a class while observing it live, and compare observation notes with the tape for accuracy.

To improve understanding of teaching and learning	Teach at least one class daily. Read current educational literature. Discuss instructional issues at faculty meetings. Take a refresher course in educational psychology or teaching methods.

To enlarge reservoir of technical ideas for teachers	Start a file on teaching methods, recording every worthwhile idea. Have teachers regularly share (in faculty meetings) new ideas they have found to be successful; record and catalog their discoveries. Read current periodicals for teachers and reviews of educational research; note teaching tips and save them in file. Observe classes taught by master teachers; record worthy methods. Experiment personally with new methods while teaching; record results.

To improve understanding of child development	Take a college course in human growth and development. Observe children of all ages; note mental, emotional, social, physical, and moral characteristics. Discuss children with a local child psychologist.

To improve understanding of supervisory functions	Read several books on supervision. Take graduate courses in principles of supervision. Brainstorm supervisory practices with other school administrators. Read current educational and leadership periodicals. Try various supervisory techniques and evaluate their effectiveness.

To improve ability to lead group activities	Take course in small-group dynamics. Participate in small-group leadership training in local church. Observe other leaders and their techniques for guiding groups to decisions. Experiment at least twice a year with new techniques for group discussions.

Supervisory excellence does not appear suddenly. It requires consistent attention and practice, as well as committed prayer. Learning supervisors should isolate specific traits or skills, attending to them until they are mastered. Regular reappraisal (perhaps each semester) is recommended.

A personal evaluation checklist (see Supervisor's Plan for Personal Development on the accompanying disk) is included to assist supervisors in organizing growth plans. This form lists the qualities and skills of good supervisors and provides space for evaluation comments and notes on personal plans for effecting improvement. Administrators should make use of this or a similar instrument in order to direct and focus their own growth strategies.

Can the Same Person Serve as Evaluator and Supervisor?

"Supervisors face a conflict since they are caught between two roles—evaluator and facilitator. Supervisors often ask, How can I help teachers grow as persons and as classroom instructors when they know that, eventually, I must make a written evaluation of their effectiveness?"[6] Some schools try to separate the roles—one administrator facilitates teacher improvement, and another makes contract evaluations. In most Christian schools, however, one person wears both hats. Even the strongest proponents of coaching strategies argue that educators must be very clear about which hat (coaching or evaluation) they are wearing when they provide feedback on teaching.[7]

Underlying issue At the core of this conflict is the issue of trust. Do the teachers trust the person performing both roles to be fair, open, honest, and sincerely concerned for their welfare? "Teachers are most threatened when they are unaware of the criteria by which they will be judged and when they do not trust the evaluator's ability to be fair," report Acheson and Gall.[8] If teachers are confident that information gathered while observing them will not be used for negative contract evaluations, the same person can perform both roles successfully. However, if teachers mistrust supervisors' motives in their classroom visits, they may hesitate to be open about their teaching difficulties.

Developing administrator-teacher trust When trust relationships exist between teachers and administrators, supervision of instruction can bring positive improvements. What does it take to establish this trust? Several administrator behaviors have been suggested:

Be clear with teachers that their success is assumed. Contract renewal is not in jeopardy unless clear advance warning has been given.

Be involved in helping teachers. Teachers should sense administrators' genuine concern for their welfare and success.

Don't blindside teachers with parent or student complaints. By using the school's Matthew 18 principle, administrators give teachers the option of resolving complaints in the least public manner.

Keep communication lines open. Teachers must feel safe enough to share openly with administrators any problems they are facing in the classroom. Administrators must avoid sending the message they are too busy to listen to teachers' needs.

Be honest about the teacher's status. Teachers must trust administrators to be truthful about their performance evaluation status. Administrators should not tell teachers that their work is satisfactory if inwardly they doubt that a new contract will be offered.

A Christian perspective Most scriptural models of leadership suggest that evaluation and assistance can be performed successfully by the same person. Government rulers, church elders, and parents are entrusted with both ruling and serving functions. God Himself provides the perfect blend of justice and mercy, of condemnation and grace, within the essence of one person.

Chapter Summary

Characteristics of good leadership fall into three primary categories: personal character qualities, interaction or relationship qualities, and organizational or managerial qualities. These qualities have parallels in biblical references to spiritual leadership as well as in research focusing on leadership in education.

For an administrator desiring to enhance his or her leadership skills, the pre-requisites are a personal walk with God and the conviction of God's calling to Christian school leadership.

Once administrators have taken inventory of their personal strengths and weaknesses, they can identify skills that need development. These may include relating to subordinates, conferencing, communication, classroom observation, knowledge of teaching and learning, awareness of technical ideas for teachers, understanding of child development, and leadership of group activities. Administrators should employ strategies and activities that foster personal development in their own areas of need.

As biblical models illustrate, when a relationship of trust exists, it is possible for the same person to evaluate teachers and to assist their professional growth.

Supervisor's Prayer

Dear Father, thank you for leading me with certainty to Christian school administration. Thank you for equipping me by your Holy Spirit to perform spiritual leadership. Grant me the insight and humility to recognize where I am weak, and the determination to find sources of strengthening. I want to be an administrator whose inadequacies do not stand in the way of your work in the school, and one whose strengths can be used in your hand as mighty tools of ministry. May Jesus Christ be glorified in me. Amen.

Endnotes

1. Blome. Unpublished study reported in "Principles of Supervision," chapter by A. C. Fortosis in *Administration of the Christian School*, Roy W. Lowrie, ed. (Colorado Springs, CO: ACSI, 1984), 101.
2. Fortosis, "Principles of Supervision," Ibid., 102.
3. Arthur Blumberg and William Greenfield, *The Effective Principal: Perspectives on School Leadership* (Boston: Allyn and Bacon, 1980).
4. Russell Gersten and Douglas Carnine, *Administrative and Supervisory Support Functions for the Implementation of Effective Educational Programs for Low Income Students* (Eugene, OR: Center for Educational Policy and Management, University of Oregon, 1981).
5. B. Sheppard, "Exploring the Transformational Nature of Instructional Leadership," *The Alberta Journal of Educational Research* 42 (1996), 327, 339.
6. Keith A. Acheson and Meredith Damien Gall, *Techniques in the Clinical Supervision of Teachers* (New York: Longman, 1997), 15. See also pages 177–179 for additional discussion of the tension between accountability and professional growth.
7. A. Costa and R. Garmston, *Cognitive Coaching: A Foundation for Renaissance Schools.* (Norwood, MA: Christopher-Gordon Publishers, 1994).
8. Acheson and Gall, 15.

Materials on Disk

Form 06 Supervisor's Plan for Personal Development

7

Effective Teaching Practices

The result was that when Jesus had finished these words, the multitudes were amazed at His teaching; for He was teaching them as one having authority, and not as their scribes.
(Matthew 7:28–29)

Chapter highlights....

Effective practices for preparing and delivering instruction
Evidences of biblical integration in teaching

Every school should have at least one administrator who knows what good teaching is! Numerous studies since the 1970s have investigated how teaching practices affect students' academic performance, classroom deportment, and attitudes toward themselves and school. This chapter summarizes the practices shown to bring positive outcomes. Supervisors can use their knowledge of these practices to choose topics for faculty training or to guide their classroom observations.

Faculty training What better topic is there for faculty in-service sessions than effective teaching practices? Administrators can identify the practices, techniques, and skills that seem to be most needed by their faculty. Then they can schedule appropriate training or discussion sessions around those needs.

Classroom observation guide Effective teaching practices can form the basis of a classroom observation instrument for supervisors to use during class visits (see chapter 11). Teachers working as peer coaches or teaching mentors can also use such an instrument effectively.

What Are Effective Teaching Practices?

Most educators have personal opinions about good teaching practices. When asked, teachers and administrators can usually list ten to fifteen teacher behaviors they consider effective—but no two lists will contain the same elements. Who is right? If school leaders want to foster good teaching, what teacher behaviors do they promote?

Since the 1970s, numerous researchers have attempted to identify those teaching practices that contribute the most to student learning. The combined effect of this research is a mosaic of pedagogical techniques and strategies that can be loosely organized into the following eleven categories:
• Preparing students to receive instruction
• Motivating students to receive and attend to instruction
• Sequencing lesson components for maximum learning
• Using review and reinforcement during and after the lesson
• Involving students actively in the lesson
• Strategically adjusting difficulty levels of a lesson
• Managing the classroom for maximum attention and participation
• Creating diverse ways for students to interact
• Using questions in a timely and effective manner
• Using instructional aids effectively
• Assessing student learning in a variety of ways and in accord with objectives

The following sections describe each of these strategies in greater detail.

Preparation of Students		
Good teachers *motivate* students to learn by ...	establishing a climate for learning	Are students focused and involved? Is an "anticipatory set" used?
	gaining students' attention	Humor, graphics, quizzes, and visuals are means of focusing student attention.
	stating what is to be learned	Knowing the lesson's objectives can be an "advance organizer" in students' cognitive structures.

Motivation of Students		
Good teachers *motivate* students to learn by ...	establishing the importance of the lesson material	Does the teacher show why the material is important, either for immediate or long-term use?
	relating new information to prior student knowledge and experiences	New information is more likely to be retained when it is linked to existing knowledge.
	using appropriate cooperative learning techniques	For many students, the opportunity to share learning with peers is a motivator.

Sequencing of Lesson Delivery		
Good teachers *sequence* delivery in logical order for learning by ...	reviewing skills basic to the new lesson	This review connects the lesson to prior learning and checks on student readiness for new material.
	presenting concrete material before abstract concepts and moving from simple to complex	When students are first confronted with abstract, complex material, confusion results and learning time is lost.
	using manipulative and visual approaches as precursors to oral explanations	This assists in drawing students into the lesson and addressing various learning modes.
	checking for student understanding at intervals by periodically reviewing lesson progress and confirming what has been learned	These practices serve to reinforce learning and indicate to teachers any reteaching that may be needed.
	using good questioning techniques	Questioning is a powerful teaching tool and should be sequenced to engage students as needed.
	using guided practice when appropriate	To assure that students know how to use the new skill, they should practice in class under the teacher's supervision.

Review and Reinforcement		
Good teachers use *review and reinforcement* of teaching by ...	immediately using guided group work	Cooperative groups can create powerful reinforcement of lesson material if they are used immediately after instruction.
	immediately using independent seatwork	Some information or skills are better reviewed through individual work.
	using homework assignments as delayed review and reinforcement	Homework assignments should connect to the lesson objectives.

Active Involvement of Students		
Good teachers *involve students actively* in learning by ...	not dominating the lesson by being the "center stage" presenter for the whole lesson	Though direct instruction is legitimate, it results in better learning when it is blended with opportunities for students to be active participants rather than passive receivers.
	inviting student contribution and response	Do teachers proactively seek student involvement? Or do they simply wait for interruptions?
	planning activities that require student involvement and initiative	Do teachers think in advance about active learning? Do they proactively plan active learning?

Difficulty Levels		
Good teachers *plan for varied difficulty levels* by ...	ensuring that skills not yet mastered are reviewed or retaught	Students should achieve an acceptable confidence level with previously taught skills before they are taught new ones.
	introducing new skills to students	Once having attained confidence with previous skills, students should be challenged with new skills.
	monitoring student learning during the lesson so as to adjust difficulty level if needed	Teachers should be ready to make mid-class decisions about the speed or level of instruction.

Classroom Management		
Good teachers *manage the classroom* well by ...	planning procedures that will reduce class disruptions	Does the teacher think ahead and plan for smooth transitions and ways of keeping students focused and involved rather than having "dead time" that opens the opportunity for students to free-lance their behavior?
	communicating rules and expectations clearly	Are the rules clear and enforceable? Are they posted along with consequences?
	being aware of all students and intercepting misbehavior at the earliest possible stage	Is the teacher aware of the whole class? Does the teacher intercept misbehavior in the least public manner so as not to distract the whole class?

Diversity of Student Interactions		
Good teachers *encourage diversity of interaction* among students by ...	structuring ways for students to speak and respond to the ideas of their peers	Some techniques include panels, role-playing, debates, simulations, and inner-outer circle discussions.
	creating opportunities for interaction to flow in ways other than teacher-to-student and vice versa	Teachers can redirect student questions or comments so that peers respond to each other.

Effective Use of Questions		
Good teachers *use questions effectively* by ...	asking fewer factual response questions and more questions that require higher order thinking such as application, analysis, or synthesis.	Questions are powerful teaching tools when students must cognitively engage in complex processing.
	ensuring that every student has time to think of a response before a question is answered	Do teachers ask questions first, pause for all students to think, and then call for a single respondent?

Effective Use of Instructional Aids		
Good teachers *use instructional aids effectively* by ...	planning how the aids will contribute to achieving the lesson objectives	For example, do teachers use audiovisuals to achieve clear learning objectives, or do they sometimes use them as "fillers"?
	planning how they will engage multiple modes or avenues of learning, such as auditory, visual, and kinesthetic	Do teachers use various instructional aids rather than relying exclusively on a favorite?
	using books and other written materials that are appropriate for lesson content and the level of the students' understanding	Do teachers review library books in advance for readability and level of difficulty?

Assessment of Learning		
Good teachers *assess student learning* by ...	aligning assessment with the course learning objectives	Do teachers use the full cycle of objectives, teaching, and assessment in a holistic manner?
	using testing as a means of guiding student improvement	Do teacher and students view tests a means of identifying areas that are not yet mastered?
	constructing assessment activities that are clear to students	Confusing tests produce invalid scores.
	using assessment activities that give students opportunities to show learning in various ways.	Do teachers employ a variety of assessment means—oral, written, projects, objective, subjective?

How Does Good Biblical Integration Show?

Supervisors working with teachers to make biblical truth a natural part of teaching and learning may look for evidence from three sources—teachers themselves, students, and the empty classroom. If biblical integration is truly in the teacher's heart and has high priority, it will show itself in all three of these. Such teachers engage in studying, thinking, and other activities that transform them over time into persons in whom biblical truth lives. But administrators do not usually see these activities. For them, the teachers' words and actions are the only indicators of biblical integration. The following are some of these actions:

Good teachers *outwardly demonstrate that biblical integration is taking place* by ...	modeling obedience to biblical principles	This is the starting point—teachers who are what they expect their students to become.
	teaching students in accord with the biblical view of the learner made in God's image	Learners made in God's image are rational, social, emotional, purposeful, active, able to make decisions, etc. Integrative teachers assume their students have these characteristics.
	referring openly to applicable biblical principles	When using secular texts, teachers must initiate the fusion of biblical truth with course content.
	giving students opportunities to develop connections between biblical truth and subject matter	Teachers create assignments and projects that require students to do their own integrative thinking.

As teachers engage in these integration-promoting activities, students will begin to think and express the unity of God's truth in all areas of study. Teachers and supervisors can look for student expressions of biblical integration in two areas—behavior and expression.

Students of good teachers *show biblical integration* by ...	applying biblical values and principles in ethical questions and behavioral situations.	Do students show they are applying biblical principles as they relate to authority, resolve conflict, show consideration, and so forth?
	showing that they understand the role of Scripture in the interpretation of scientific theories, historical events, literature, etc.	Students speak with integrative understanding regarding creation v. evolution, God's role in the history of nations, the role of literature, etc.

Finally, even with no one present, the classroom should give evidence that the teacher is integrating well! On display will be bulletin boards and wall postings that provoke students to think analytically about biblical truth in the subject area. There will also be samples of original student work that reveal students' understanding of biblical integration. In summary, if biblical integration is central in teachers' hearts, it will show in their personal demeanor, in their teaching and relating to students, in the students themselves, and in their classrooms.

Chapter Summary

Research reveals certain pedagogical practices that are effective in improving student learning and attitudes. These practices encompass planning, setting objectives, involving students, asking questions, sequencing lessons, using review and reinforcement, pacing instruction, managing the classroom, and assessing student learning. In addition, Christian school teachers should themselves be biblical integrators as they educate students to place biblical principles at the core of all learning and living.

Administrators may refer to these practices during faculty training. In addition, they can use them in constructing instruments for classroom observation and summative evaluation.

Supervisor's Prayer

Dear Lord, I thank you for the wonderful model of teaching excellence given by our Savior. I pray that I may be your instrument to assist our faculty in becoming teachers after your own heart. We want to teach well and do it to your glory. We want our teaching to be in line with the way you have created students to learn. Thank you for the wisdom you will give as we immerse ourselves in your Word. In the name of Jesus I pray. Amen.

Endnotes

For discussions of research on teacher effectiveness, the author recommends the following resources:

T. Good, "Teaching Effects and Teacher Evaluation," *Second Handbook of Research on Teacher Education*, J. Sikula, ed. (New York: Macmillan, 1996), 617–665.

Keith A. Acheson and Meredith Damien Gall, *Techniques in the Clinical Supervision of Teachers* (New York: Longman, 1997), 23–47.

Materials on Disk

Classroom observation forms based on effective teaching practices are included with the materials for chapter 11, "Classroom Observations."

8

Motivating Teachers Toward Improvement

*For it is God who is at work in you, both to
will and to work for His good pleasure.*
Philippians 2:13

Chapter highlights....

Motivation theories
A motivation model for Christian teachers
Strategies for motivating teachers
Motivating across age groups and cultures

Frustrated and bewildered, the veteran administrator leaned back in her chair and stared at the ceiling. She had been supervising a young teacher for five years. Throughout that time, the teacher had continued to exhibit the same teaching and performance deficiencies. Countless observations and evaluations had been conducted. Conferences had been held. The result? Little or no perceptible improvement. No wonder the administrator puzzled, "Why can't I get him to change?"

Administrators will realize the complexities buried in this situation. Human motivation is not easily described or analyzed, nor can it be controlled with precision. There is no "cookbook formula" that can be applied universally. Yet a supervisor's success depends largely on motivating teachers to improve.

This chapter highlights important aspects of Christian school teacher motivation. The goal is to provide administrators with a framework for understanding teacher motivation and to suggest tactics for increasing motivation in all teachers.

How Do Motivation Theories Relate to Christian School Teachers?

Maslow's hierarchy of needs

The well-known psychologist Abraham Maslow theorized that human motivation is dependent on the satisfaction of needs.[1] He arranged those needs in a hierarchical order and suggested that the lowest need that is not being satisfied becomes a person's motivator. The following chart lists the needs from highest to lowest, or most basic.

Need Level	Satisfiers for Teachers
Self-actualization	Self and peer recognition; responsibility; achievement seen as creative change for the better
Esteem (ego status)	Prestige; informal leader; chairperson
Love (belongingness)	Social gatherings; faculty committees; teacher organizations
Safety	Job security; contract; tenure
Basic needs	Job; salary

For example, teachers whose income is inadequate for their family's health needs or for emergency expenses are not going to be motivated by the need for personal fulfillment. The lower, more powerful needs must be satisfied first. Thus administrators may find it difficult to appeal successfully to their teachers' desire for professional improvement if salaries or medical insurance plans are inadequate.

Christians recognize in this theory a certain ring of truth. Jesus often satisfied people's physical needs for healing or food before He shared the gospel message. At the same time, the Christian view does not require that lower order needs always be met before higher order needs can become motivators. For instance, the Bible does not require that hunger be satisfied or diseases healed before a person is motivated by spiritual need. The thief on the cross acted out of his spiritual deficiency in spite of severe physiological and safety needs.

The most serious difference between Maslow's perspective and a Christian one is the issue of who defines *need*. For Maslow, humans determine their needs, but for a Christian, God's definition of *need* is the real one. Our human needs are real only if God considers them real, and in God's hierarchy, our greatest need is spiritual. Jesus teaches us to "seek first His kingdom and His righteousness; and all these things shall be added to you" (Matthew 6:33). The spiritual need transcends all others because it concerns eternal matters rather than temporal ones.

Thus a Christian view suggests that teachers' primary motivation should flow from a desire to fulfill their spiritual need to seek first God's kingdom and His righteousness. Christian teachers should not depend for their motivation on the kind of need satisfaction that Maslow posits. On the other hand, Christian school boards and administrators should follow Christ's example by seeking to meet their teachers' lower-level needs. They should not depend on spiritual motivation alone to keep teachers in a school that pays inadequate salaries and ignores basic needs.

Hertzberg's two-factor theory

Like Maslow, Frederick Hertzberg saw motivation as related to satisfaction, but instead of need satisfaction he proposed job satisfaction. According to Hertzberg, factors that cause dissatisfaction are related to the job environment. They may include working conditions, status, job security, salary, technical supervision, and company policies. When these do not live up to their expectations, employees are dissatisfied.

On the other hand, satisfaction (or motivation) is derived from the work itself and the achievement, recognition, advancement, and responsibility it brings.[2] As applied to Christian schools, Hertzberg's theory suggests that teachers are dissatisfied only if certain conditions in the job environment are deficient, and that the presence of those conditions will motivate them to better performance. As with Maslow's ideas, there is partial truth here.

Christian school teachers generally do not count on working conditions, salary, status, or benefits to give them job satisfaction. They are more likely to gain fulfillment from the work itself and the results they see in students. Fortified with a sense of calling, Christian school teachers may endure deficiencies in the job environment patiently until those deficiencies create so much discomfort that they become dissatisfied.

For Christian school teachers, material concerns become motivators at contract time when they must decide whether the salary and benefits offered are adequate. Once they answer this question, teachers enter Christian school teaching with full knowledge of the financial ground rules. They do not count on pay increases to motivate them toward professional improvement.

Both laboratory researchers and educators in the field agree that extrinsic motivators, such as pay increases and improved benefits, do not promote professional and personal growth.[3] In studies by Deci and associates, adults who were rewarded for tasks the first time they performed them showed decreased levels of performance when they worked on the same tasks a second time without mention of reward. Another group of adults, who worked with no promise of reward, tended to return to their tasks the second time with more enthusiasm and commitment than the rewarded group had shown.[4]

As applied to Christian school teachers, this research suggests that external motivators that administrators use to improve teacher performance can actually result in lackluster performance if the motivators are later withdrawn or overlooked. Teachers may sense that administrators view them, in behaviorist terms, as responders to stimuli rather than as concerned, internally-motivated professionals. It appears that administrators seeking instructional improvement would be wise to appeal to teachers' *intrinsic motivation*, their personal desire to please God and perform His work with excellence.

How Should Christian Teachers' Motivation Be Viewed?

In analyzing a topic as complex as motivation, it may be helpful to develop a theoretical framework, identifying both positive and negative influences on teacher motivation. When positive influences outweigh negative ones, teacher motivation is high, just as it is low when negative influences outweigh the positive ones. The supervisory strategy becomes one of heightening faculty motivation by increasing the positive influences and reducing the negative interferers, as seen in the following schematic.

positive contributors	*plus*	negative detractors	*results in*	teacher motivation level

The following discussion describes positive and negative influences in more detail:

Positive Contributors to Teacher Motivation

1. **The Holy Spirit's indwelling** Since the Holy Spirit indwells Christian teachers, their conscience pulls them toward doing their best for God's glory. If the Holy Spirit is given permanent control, teachers will be willing to change their teaching behavior in order to enhance their work for God.

Though this ideal rarely exists, administrators can rejoice that their teachers have supernatural power within them.

2. **A calling from God to teach** Though not all Christian teachers have sensed God's call, the great majority have. These have an added incentive to perform with excellence, making their administrators' motivational task easier. Recently, motivational psychologists have validated the importance of the intrinsic motivation derived from meaningful work. Two rules emerge from their research: (1) what is rewarding gets done, and (2) what teachers believe in and think to be good gets done.[5]

3. **An assumption that improvement is always possible** No teacher has achieved perfection. Every teacher should say, "I can always do better." This assumption motivates teachers toward improvement and excellence.

4. **A love for students** Teachers who sincerely love students will want to provide classroom experiences that result in learning and growth. Thus, teachers who believe that new or different teaching techniques are in their students' best interest are more open to innovation than teachers who have little love for students.

5. **Perception of oneself as a professional** Teachers who perceive themselves as mature, concerned professionals are apt to seek pedagogical improvement. Professional teachers do not permit themselves to stagnate when better ways of teaching are available.

Negative Influences on Motivation

1. **The basic human nature** Christian school teachers must reckon with their human nature, which tends toward laziness, mediocrity, and personal comfort. To the extent that the old nature is in control, a teacher's motivation to teach with excellence in order to glorify God will be blunted. Supervisors may find themselves fighting this foe as they seek to help teachers improve.

2. **The difficulty of changing established habits** Most behaviors that teachers exhibit are not new to them but are learned, repeated behaviors that have become habits. Because habits are comfortable, teachers may not be willing to change them and create temporary psychological "discomfort." Administrators need to realize that replacing old habits with new ones may take months. Requiring teachers to make numerous major changes quickly

can cause enough "pain" that teachers will find excuses for avoiding the changes.

3. **The perception that changing is an overwhelming task** Teachers who see pedagogical improvement as a monumental process may give up before starting. A college president had attended a semester's first round of classes. He realized that the students now felt deluged with assignments, papers, and exams. His simple advice? "Things will look up if they are looked after." The task appeared so great that many were tempted to conclude that they'd already lost the academic battle, but the president's words boosted their motivation by making the task seem manageable. Teachers' motivation to improve is enhanced when they see improvement as a manageable possibility.

4. **The influence of fatigue** Teachers in Christian schools are often assigned multiple class preparations along with numerous other duties. This combination drains their mental, emotional, physical, and spiritual energy. They become so pressed merely to keep up with each day's demands that their only motivation is to survive. There is no time or creative energy available to devote to improvement, and their thoughts are consumed with staying thirty minutes ahead of the next task. Administrators must be sensitive to the influence of fatigue from over-demand and find little ways to relieve such pressures so that teachers can plan improvement activities with reasonable vigor.

What Strategies Motivate Teachers?

First-level strategies

According to the theoretical model described above, an administrator's primary method of motivating teachers is to increase the positive influences and decrease the negative ones. Here are some ways of doing so:

1. **Praying for teachers** Administrators should rely first on the power of God's Holy Spirit in Christian teachers. Universally, administrators see that praying for their teachers is necessary, but in actual practice prayer may be secondary. One way for administrators to reverse this trend is to use their teachers' annual improvement goals as "prayer card" reminders. Calling on God's power, daily and systematically, to change teachers should be each administrator's first priority for improving the quality of instruction.

2. **Creating a trusting, supportive environment** When teachers are confident that an administrator is on their side, they do not imagine a hidden agenda behind every classroom visit. They have less resistance to change and receive supervision as a positive, friendly operation that provides genuine assistance.

3. **Making change manageable** Sometimes teachers cannot focus on specific improvements because the number of changes needed is so great. Administrators must encourage such teachers to concentrate on one improvement goal at a time and to incorporate new teaching ideas into their repertoires gradually. Supervisors who visit classes once a year and stockpile their improvement suggestions may sabotage teacher motivation by making the task appear overwhelming.

4. **Using influence levels appropriate for each teacher** Administrators may employ several levels of assertiveness (influence) as motivational tools. (These levels are described in the Additional Strategies section that follows.) In doing so, they should match their tactics to their teachers' existing motivation levels, from high to low. Mismatches may retard motivation. For example, using indirect, passive techniques with low-motivation teachers may have so little effect that whatever motivation exists may be lulled into deeper stagnation. In contrast, active and coercive measures may dampen the enthusiasm of teachers who are already highly motivated for instructional improvement. A wise match between technique and teacher is required. For most teachers, these four tactics will be enough to enhance motivation.

Additional Strategies

Thus administrators who desire to improve teacher motivation should match their supervisory styles to the needs of their individual teachers. In terms of administrative influence, these supervisory styles range from "passive" to "coercive." Passive tactics rely on existing teacher motivation, whereas coercive tactics attempt to create motivation where it is lacking.

1. **Exposing teachers to good teaching ideas (passive; high motivation exists)** All that is needed for teachers with high personal motivation is to let them know about good teaching techniques. They are eager to improve their classroom practices. By bringing in outside educators to make presentations, holding special in-service sessions, allowing teachers to visit other classes or schools, placing interest centers in the faculty lounge, or sending teachers to teacher conventions, administrators may provide

sparks that will ignite fires of instructional change.

2. **Planning for interaction regarding teaching ideas (passive; good motivation exists)** You can turn teacher motivation up a notch by planning faculty sessions around discussions or debates about innovative teaching ideas:

   a. Faculty members who have used certain methods successfully can describe or demonstrate them for others and then answer questions about them.

   b. Curriculum reviews allow for faculty discussion of different teaching methods.

   c. Accreditation studies involving the full faculty can spur teachers on to implement improvements in their classes.

3. **Making supervision a collaborative venture (passive/active; average motivation)** In this mode, supervisors and teachers assume equally active roles in suggesting and promoting improvement. During such collaboration, teachers are likely to extend their comfort zones voluntarily and try promising new ideas, for they sense support and encouragement from their supervisors. The clinical supervision model (chapter 5) lends itself to this tactic.

4. **Suggesting specific changes to specific teachers (active; fair motivation)** Teachers whose motivational levels are not very high are unlikely to respond to passive supervision, so for them administrators may need to suggest specific improvements. An administrator's individual attention and concern increases the teacher's sense of the urgency of change. Such tactics will motivate teachers only if they and their supervisors already share a trust relationship.

5. **Requiring specific changes (coercive; low motivation)** As a final step, administrators may need to insist that certain teachers make specific pedagogical changes. Admittedly, this is the most coercive and least desirable tactic because it admits that the teachers' own motivation is inadequate. In such cases, coercion is usually linked with "intensive correction" status, which in turn suggests that contract renewal is in jeopardy.

Motivating Teachers of Various Age Groups and Cultures

When dealing with teacher motivation, administrators should take into account the experiences and viewpoints of persons from generations or cultures other than their own. Many strategies suggested in this book rely on teachers' positive responses to a gentle blend of authority and collaboration.

Such a foundation grows out of biblical principles, but it is also characteristic of American relational patterns in the late 20th and early 21st centuries. Not all age groups or cultural groups are comfortable with this paradigm.

Cultural considerations International or missions school administrators who supervise a culturally and racially mixed faculty must be aware of possible influences on the effectiveness of their supervisory style. These influences, identified in a 1997 Christian school administrator conference for schools in Asia, include the following:

- Persons from some cultures tend to be quiet in group discussions, rarely speaking out aggressively as Americans do.
- Persons from some cultures prefer to listen and be taught. For them, learning through active participation is neither natural nor preferred.
- Teachers from some cultures prefer a didactic, teacher-centered approach rather than a student centered, activity-oriented one.
- Teachers from some cultures prefer that supervisors relate to them in hierarchical fashion, telling them how to improve. For these teachers to accept peer coaching and collaboration, careful training and gentle leadership is required.
- For teachers from most cultures, trust relationships with supervisors and peer group members are very important.[6]

Administrators in such schools must be sensitive to these and other cultural differences. They should study carefully how best to apply biblical principles of supervision in their schools. If they determine that changes in their teachers' usual approaches to relationships will result in better Christian education, they should proceed only in the context of a strong base of trust. International schools that successfully introduce new modes of supervision and interaction to culturally diverse faculties do so with careful prayer, sensitivity, and gentle training.

Age-group considerations What do mature administrators need to know about supervising teachers born a generation or more after them? The radical shifts in American culture between the 1950s and the present have created subcultures linked loosely to the eras or decades in which their members were born and reared. Christian school teachers are not immune to the influences of these subcultures. The following chart offers suggestions for supervising teachers of different age groups.[7]

Generation	Birth Years	Characteristics	Supervision Suggestions
Older Adults Silent Generation	1927–1942	• Traditional • Responds to process-driven leadership • Accepts positional authority	• Can be outstanding resource • Capitalize on grandfather-type roles • Give them a sense of worthwhile contribution • Comfortable with formal assessment
Baby Boomers	1943–1962	• Responds to visionary, confident leadership • Likes small groups • Accepts diversity	• Give practical, rather than theoretical help • Encourage them to progress to next level • Challenge them to be mentors • Give opportunities to discuss issues in groups
Generation X	1963–1978	• Authority must be earned • Genuine, caring social relationships • Responds best to consultative, pragmatic, cautious leadership	• Provide positive reinforcement and assurance of self-worth • Identify small list of essential requirements • Encourage personal journaling about teaching
Generation Next	1979–1989	• Enjoys participation and relationships • Responds to grand, expansive leadership • Learns from others • Is influenced by postmodernism's plurality	• Use peer coaching • Focus on biblical truth in school's curriculum and practice • Schedule opportunities to interact with administration and board

Chapter Summary

This chapter has described certain assumptions about teachers and the influences on their motivation for professional growth. Supervisors should have both an overall strategy and specific tactics for improving teacher motivation.

The following schematic reviews the relationships of concepts in this chapter. Specific methods for carrying out these strategies are amplified in other chapters.

Factors Affecting Motivation		plus	Supervisory Strategies	yield	Results
Positive	Negative		• Trust relationships • Making change manageable • Using right influence levels • Presenting good ideas • Creating teacher interaction about ideas • Teacher-supervisor collaboration • Suggesting specific changes • Requiring specific changes		Teacher motivation levels
• Holy Spirit • Calling • Improvement possible • Love for students • Self-perception as professional	• Human nature • Changing habits • Change too overwhelming • Fatigue from excessive demands				

In addition, administrators should attend to the assumptions they find in teachers from various cultures and age groups.

Supervisor's Prayer

Dear Lord, how grateful I am that You know our frames, that you understand each teacher and administrator intimately. Therefore, I call on you for your wisdom in helping my teachers want to improve. I ask you to give me insight into their needs and thoughts so that I can help them minister to students as you desire them to. And search me also, Lord. Know my thoughts, and reveal to me the motives of my heart. In the name of Jesus, Amen.

Endnotes

1. Abraham H. Maslow, *Motivation and Personality* (New York: Harper and Row, 1954).
2. F. Hertzberg, B. Mausner, and B. Snyderman, *The Motivation in Work* (New York: Wiley, 1959).
3. Carl Glickman, Stephen Gordon, and Jovita Ross-Gordon, *Supervision of Instruction: A Developmental Approach* (Boston: Allyn and Bacon, 1998), 196.
4. E. L. Deci, "Motivation," Paper presented to the annual meeting of the Midwest Association of Teachers of Educational Psychology (Dayton, Ohio: 30 October 1982).
5. Thomas J. Sergiovanni, "Why Should We Seek Substitutes for Leadership?" *Educational Leadership* 49 (February 1992), 45.
6. Notes collected at MCOS-ACSI conference (Malaysia, November 1997).
7. Assembled from notes collected at MCOS-ACSI conference (Malaysia, November 1997) and sheet compiled by Lee Cook and Marlene LeFever (Colorado Springs, CO: David C. Cook Publishing Co, 1998).

9

Tools for Teacher Self-Improvement

*For if I do this willingly, I have a reward; but if against
my will, I have been entrusted with a stewardship.*
(1 Corinthians 9:17)

Chapter highlights....

Use of student evaluations
Peer coaching and mentoring
Videotaping

A Christian school study in 1982 revealed that principals who treat teachers as mature, concerned professionals are likely to see positive effects on faculty unity.[1] The study also showed that teachers respond well when administrators involve them in decisions impacting school improvement. Such a supervisory policy appeals to teachers' intrinsic motivation, a desire to please God and do His work with excellence. The implied assumptions about Christians are congruent with biblical principles. (See chapter 8, "Motivating Teachers Toward Improvement.")

Similarly, treating teachers as mature, concerned professionals is likely to create a climate in which teachers initiate self-improvement. When administrators encourage teachers to evaluate their instructional practice, and when they equip their faculty with the time, equipment, expertise, and personnel to carry out improvement plans, they manifest confidence in teachers which, in turn, generates improved instruction.

This chapter will discuss three tools that administrators can use to facilitate teacher self-improvement—student evaluations, peer coaching and mentoring, and videotaping classes.

Student Evaluations

It may first be proper to change the term "student evaluations" to "student feedback." *Evaluation* suggests judgments made by supervisors; *feedback* implies the reflection of oneself in a mirror. The use of student feedback is not without controversy, for the practice has limitations as well as advantages that administrators should balance thoughtfully when considering its use in teacher self-assessment.

Limitations Among the drawbacks to using student feedback are:

1. **Perception of influence** Students may assume that they can influence dismissal decisions on unpopular teachers, especially if written student feedback is rarely requested. Infrequent requests for student feedback may attract undue attention, and students may attribute to themselves a sense of false power. One way to neutralize this drawback is to encourage all teachers to request student feedback every year as a routine source of information for personal improvement.

2. **Immaturity of perspective** Students who perceive certain teachers as too demanding are often heard several years later praising those same teachers. The passage of time and a broader perspective change students' evaluation of earlier school experiences. Teacher qualities that are undervalued by thirteen-year-olds are often valued highly five or six years later. Thus, in using student feedback, one must consider the impact of student immaturity. Perhaps the best way to reduce that impact is to structure evaluation questions so that they call for objective ratings of observable teacher behaviors and practices. Notice, for example, the difference in rater subjectivity required by the following statements.

Statement: If you do not understand something, is your teacher willing to help?
Revision: Does your teacher help you when you request it?
Does your teacher ask you whether you understand something that was taught?

Statement: Is your teacher interesting?
Revision: Does your teacher plan interesting class activities?
Does your teacher talk enthusiastically?

3. **"Halo" and "horns" effect** Strange terms? Maybe, but they represent the tendency of evaluators to rate teachers uniformly high or uniformly low on

all characteristics, depending on the raters' general impressions. Certainly students are not immune to this tendency. If they have generally positive impressions of a teacher, students may give high marks to homework, classroom management, testing, and instructional clarity. Conversely, students may rate unpopular teachers low on all qualities. Such evaluations, whether high or low, do not provide the feedback teachers need in order to structure some improvement goals. Though this effect cannot be totally eliminated, it can be reduced by creating rating categories that identify practices that students see and experience rather than what they feel.

Statement: Does your teacher like you?
Revision: Does your teacher do things that prove she likes you?
Does your teacher smile when she talks to you?

Statement: Is your classroom orderly and quiet?
Revision: Does your teacher permit students to talk out of turn?
Does your teacher post classroom rules for students to read?
Does your teacher correct misbehaving students?

Advantages Despite these drawbacks, student feedback on teacher performance does have advantages:

1. **Broad sampling of input** By getting feedback from entire classes, teachers garner information from various perspectives—male and female; advanced learners and learners with difficulties; students from single-parent homes and from two-parent homes; visual, auditory, and kinesthetic learners; spiritually committed and spiritually immature students; emotionally mature and emotionally underdeveloped. The more heterogeneous the class mixture, the more reliable will be the significantly high or low ratings on specific areas of teacher performance. For example, if a class contained a good mixture of visual, auditory, and kinesthetic learners who collectively gave the teacher high marks in presentation of clear, understandable lessons, the teacher could deduce that her instruction was effective for a cross-section of learning modalities. Since teachers usually receive feedback from administrators and parents, student input provides the perspective of those experiencing the classroom environment firsthand.

2. **Exposure of "blind" areas** Information known to students but unknown to teachers may surface through student feedback. If many students perceive something about a teacher's performance or methodology of which the teacher is not aware, the teacher should investigate the matter further. A good follow-up would be to arrange for a class to be videotaped or observed by a peer teacher.

Research results Most studies involving student evaluations of teachers have been conducted at the high school and college levels. Even so, findings from selected research are noteworthy:

A 1982 study of college students and instructors concluded that (1) student personality characteristics did not have a significant relationship on their rating of instructors, (2) students perceived their teachers' personality traits as related to their effectiveness, and (3) teacher effects on student ratings were significantly greater than teacher effects on student achievement.[2] One inference for the elementary and secondary levels may be that students tend to equate teacher personality traits with teaching effectiveness. A second inference is that students' ratings of their teachers will vary far more than their achievement, suggesting the caution that student evaluations have more to do with the teaching processes than with the learning outcomes.

Another study suggests that a valid way of obtaining evaluation of teachers is to ask for students' perceptions of their progress toward educational goals that teachers have clearly determined and announced. This approach focuses more on instructional outcomes than on teachers' behaviors or processes they may use while conducting classes.[3]

A 1986 study reported that high school student ratings of student progress toward instructional goals and of teacher behaviors were similar to teachers' ratings of the same elements.[4] This outcome suggests that, at least in high school, student feedback on these dimensions was valid.

In a 1997 study with high school students and teachers in north Florida, students completed evaluation forms twice a year for each teacher, with teachers receiving feedback one week after the evaluations. Teachers were generally positive about the process and felt that voluntary participation would contribute to the usefulness of the student ratings and comments.[5]

Elementary student feedback For the most part, primary grade students will report their general impressions or feelings about teachers, but they will not be as accurate as middle school students in specifying frequency of teacher behaviors. For this reason, teachers may choose to ask them openly how they feel about such matters as teacher fairness, classroom control, clarity of instruction, and teacher helpfulness. The understanding, then, is that at the elementary level, student feedback will be general rather than specific or clinical.

Suggestions for Implementation

Here are some ideas for the use of student feedback in teacher self-evaluation:

Timeliness Gather feedback soon enough that it can be put to good use in the current school year.

Universality In a given class, request input from all students.

Specificity Structure the feedback questionnaire so that students describe specific behaviors, procedures, or outcomes rather than general impressions.

Cooperation Use of student feedback instruments by teachers should be voluntary. It is desirable, however, for an entire faculty to agree that all teachers will request such feedback.

Confidentiality The results of student feedback questionnaires should remain the personal property of teachers. Teachers may voluntarily share the data with their supervisors as part of the professional growth and development process.

Consistency Student feedback is less threatening to teachers if it is collected yearly from all students and classes.

Peer Coaching and Mentoring

In addition to student feedback, peer coaching and mentoring can provide teachers with constructive evaluations without fear of supervisory judgment. This tool is especially valuable in schools where administrators are teaching much of the day and have little time for classroom observation.

Peer coaching and mentoring can be approached with two models. The first model, coaching, places teachers in collaborative problem-solving relationships within trusting environments. They provide each other with descriptive classroom feedback in order to improve the performance of each teacher.[6] In the second model, mentoring, veteran teachers are paired with novice teachers to provide the novice with regular mentoring.[7]

Implementing the coaching model Before administrators who are hard-pressed for supervisory time jump on the bandwagon of collaborative peer coaching, they should carefully consider what is necessary for a successful program. Experience and research have shown several features that are likely to enhance the success of the teachers-coaching-teachers approach.

1. **Advance training** Teachers who will be observing each other's classes should be oriented to good practices of observation and data collection. They should be equipped with such skills as (1) how to collect data while

observing a class, (2) how to design instruments for data collection, and (3) how to interpret data. This training may be given by administrators, experienced teachers, or other professional educators. (See chapter 11, "Classroom Observations," for detailed information.) The advance training should also orient teachers to conferencing skills needed to produce a collegial atmosphere when reviewing and interpreting the data. Of course, the teachers' common Christian commitment contributes heavily to success. (See chapter 10, "Principles for Conferencing with Teachers.")

2. **Resource support**   Not only will teachers need expertise; they will need time and possibly equipment. A serious complaint of teachers who have been involved in peer coaching programs is that they had "no time" for pre-observation conferences and felt "harried" with their daily schedules. How can time be reserved for pre- and post-observation conferences between teachers? Administrators may consider the following ideas:
   • Setting aside occasional faculty meeting time for conferences regarding observations.
   • Starting school late or dismissing early on selected and pre-announced days.
   • Using volunteer aides or parents to supervise lunch or play periods.
   • Giving peer coaches the same preparation period to allow for conferencing.
   • Budgeting for substitutes to free teachers to visit each other's classes.

Finding additional time for teachers to concentrate on non-teaching tasks is always difficult, but administrators committed to collaborative supervision among teachers must be creative in making such programs possible.

In addition to time, teachers will find that videotaping is an excellent aid to making discoveries about themselves as teachers. Administrative support for purchasing camcorders will be necessary. If administrators cannot purchase them through normal budgeting, they should approach special groups—parent-teacher fellowships or other booster organizations—about purchasing equipment as a service to their schools.

3. **Appropriate structure**   Finally, administrators should structure collaborative supervision so that it is manageable and beneficial for teachers. To assure its effectiveness, administrators should:
   • pair teachers who are already, or can easily become, comfortable with each other
   • if possible, pair teachers who share the same or nearly the same grade levels
   • schedule time to review program effectiveness with all teachers
   • make peer coaching voluntary but encourage teachers to participate

Implementing the mentoring model   Mentoring is a one-way process that calls for veteran teachers to mentor beginning teachers. It requires many of the same elements as the two-way model—training, time, social comfort, and resources.

The special advantage of the mentoring approach is that one teacher is the recognized expert and the other the novice. This advance understanding eliminates some of the social uncertainty created when two equals compete over how much "help" they give to their partners.

This same advantage, however, can become a liability if new teachers feel threatened or judged by critical or insensitive mentors. To avoid this potential problem, administrators need to be certain that all the teachers involved have received training in observing classrooms, analyzing data, and conferencing. A good idea is for veteran and rookie teachers is to go through this training together.

Unlike peer coaching, mentoring is not always voluntary. For example, the school's supervision plan may require first year teachers to be mentored by an experienced faculty member. The requirement may apply to any teacher, regardless of experience level, who is in an "intensive corrective" period. On the other hand, teachers who volunteer to be mentored should certainly be supported in their request.

Videotaping

A third tool for teacher self-improvement, videotaping, is rarely used in Christian schools. In fact, in a 1990 survey of seventy-five Christian school administrators, only ten percent said they ever used videotaping as a supervisory tool.[8] Yet videotaping is the best way to preserve an objective record of classroom events. The camcorder captures sights and sounds more completely than any other means of data collection, leaving no question whether or not a certain event happened.

Videotaping has additional advantages. It allows teachers to see themselves as students see them, thus providing them with a valuable self-learning experience.[9] Their movements, expressions, mannerisms, idiosyncrasies, and gestures are captured on tape. In addition, they can hear their voice, complete with inflection, tonality, projection, and clarity. *Uh*'s and *OK*'s are dutifully recorded.

Guidelines for videotaping The approaches to videotaping are as numerous as the administrators and teachers who use the method. In line with supervision's goal of instructional improvement, Christian school administrators should consider employing it only for teacher self-review and evaluation, never for judgmental or summative purposes. With this standard in mind, the following guidelines are offered:

1. **Teacher preparation** Because some teachers are uneasy at the prospect of being videotaped, they should experiment with videotape equipment in advance. Supervisors should show them how tapes can easily be erased. As teachers gain familiarity with videotape equipment and its use, their anxiety will lessen.

Another way to prepare teachers is to alert them to natural responses they are likely to exhibit. Normally spontaneous and self-confident teachers may experience unusual anxiety and self-consciousness at the prospect of being videotaped. Their focus often moves from "How do I teach?" to "How do I look?" When teachers first view videotapes of themselves, they tend to focus on the cosmetics of their performance (e.g., physical appearance, clothes, and voice quality). By warning teachers of these likely reactions, administrators can help them approach videotaping calmly and professionally.

2. **Student preparation** Teachers in grades four through twelve should notify students in advance when video cameras will be used in their classroom. It may be advantageous to place a camera in the room for two days in advance of the taping in order to reduce the effect of its novelty. This conditioning may not be as necessary for students in kindergarten through grade three, since younger students tend to lose interest in a classroom visitor and revert to normal behavior.

3. **Equipment set-up** No longer is a vast array of equipment needed. A light tripod and a fist-sized camcorder are all it takes. Playback can be done on any television set, and the price of the equipment is well within the means of most schools. The camcorder and tripod should be placed in a location, usually at the rear or side of the classroom, that does not interfere with normal traffic and that reduces the risk of inadvertent equipment damage. If the room is large, it is wise to experiment with sound projection and microphone pick-up capabilities before the taping session.

4. **Actual taping** While taping, camera operators should continuously camera-scan the whole class, stopping occasionally to focus on the teacher. Operators should attempt to record a wide sampling of student behaviors in a variety of situations—lectures, seatwork, discussions, group activities, quizzes, the start and finish of classes. Such records will be invaluable to teachers when, in later tape reviews, they see student behaviors they had not noticed. Experience has shown that a camera often sights student actions unnoticed by teachers—hit-

ting a classmate, passing notes, whispering, lighting a match, or doodling. Since teachers' voices are recorded regardless of where the camera is focused, it is unnecessary to aim cameras continuously on the teacher.

Other useful tips on camcorder use include:
a. Fasten the camcorder securely to the tripod.
b. Remove the lens cap and aim the camcorder away from direct light.
c. Adjust the viewfinder and focus on an object approximately twenty feet away.
d. Never point at direct sunlight or strong artificial or reflected light. The color pickup element will be damaged.
e. Make sure the object being recorded is well lighted.
f. When "panning" the room, do not make sudden or quick camera moves.

5. **Camera operators** Camera operators should be educators who enjoy trust relationships with the teachers being taped. They should be educators because they must come with built-in understandings of classroom dynamics. They should enjoy trust relationships with teachers so as to reduce artificiality and stiltedness in teachers' on-camera behavior. Usually, camera operators will be administrators, supervisors, or peer teachers. Another option is to use volunteer retired teachers.

6. **Ownership of tapes** Classroom tapes should be the property of the teachers whose classes are taped. Teachers should never fear that tapes will be used in determining whether a contract will be issued. In fact, it may be appropriate for teachers to supply their own blank tapes. In this way, they can use the same tape for several classroom tapings and for subsequent self-evaluation and review. What a special delight it can be for teachers to step back in time and review their performances from earlier years! They are certain to appreciate their own growth and improvement.

7. **Reviews of tapes** Initially, teachers should review tapes in privacy to ascertain personal strengths and areas for improvement. A checklist of features to observe can be a helpful instrument. This could be the same as, or similar to, the instrument used by peer teachers or supervisors for in-person classroom observation. (See chapter 11, "Classroom Observations.") Following their personal tape reviews, teachers should discuss important observations and improvement ideas with professional peers or supervisors. A joint review of the tapes can sometimes be a mutually agreeable exercise. Such reviews have a precision of diagnosis equivalent to individual tutoring of students.[10]

Chapter Summary

Summary of Teacher Self-Improvement Roles

Self-Improvement Tool	Administrator Tasks	Teacher Tasks
Student Feedback	1. Encourage all teachers to use it every year 2. Suggest feedback instruments that call for objective data	1. Use student feedback in developing improvement goals 2. Be open to learning new things about one's teaching
Peer Coaching	1. Structure time for teacher-to-teacher conferences 2. Provide training in observing, analyzing, and conferencing 3. Acquire resources needed	1. Participate wholeheartedly 2. Expect to contribute; expect to learn
Videotaping	1. Provide forms for teachers to use when viewing tapes 2. Be available to serve as a camera operator 3. Acquire camcorder for school	1. Arrange date and camera operator for videotaping of own class 2. Bring blank tape 3. Review tape in private; record data to analyze and set improvement goals 4. Share findings, if appropriate, with peer mentor or administrator

Supervisor's Prayer

Dear Lord, how I praise you for the dedicated teachers on our faculty. They are people who love you and are called to your work. I thank you that they have a great desire to do your work in this school with excellence. Now grant me, I pray, the wisdom and sensitivity to create the opportunities and climate in which their desires to improve may blossom into fruitfulness. Thank you for receiving my prayer in Jesus' name. Amen.

Endnotes

1. Gordon B. Brown, "Leader Behavior and Faculty Cohesiveness in Christian Schools." Doctoral dissertation (Miami, FL: University of Miami, 1982).
2. Philip C. Abrami et al., "The Relationship Between Student Personality Characteristics, Teacher Ratings, and Student Achievement," *Journal of Educational Psychology* (1982), 111–125.
3. Gerald S. Hanna, "Discriminant and Convergent Validity of High School Student Ratings of Instruction," *Educational and Psychological Measurement* (1983), 873–878.
4. Judith D. Albrecht et al., "A Comparison of High School Student Ratings of Teacher Effectiveness with Teacher Self-Ratings: Factor Analytic and Multitrait-Multimethod Analysis," *Educational and Psychological Measurement* (1986), 223–231.
5. Craig A. Mertler, "Students as Stakeholders in Teacher Evaluation: Teacher Perceptions of a Formative Feedback Model." Paper presented at the Annual Meeting of the Mid-Western Educational Research Association (Chicago, IL, October 15–18, 1997).
6. Shirley A. McFaul and James M. Cooper, "Peer Clinical Supervision in an Urban Elementary School," *Journal of Teacher Education* (1983), 34–38.
7. Michael M. Fagan and Glen Walter, "Mentoring Among Teachers," *Journal of Educational Research* (1982), 113–117.
8. From survey conducted during Summer 1990 at Grace Theological Seminary, Winona Lake, IN.
9. Keith A. Acheson and Meredith Gamien Gall, *Techniques in the Clinical Supervision of Teachers* (New York: Coughman, Inc, 1980).
10. Timothy Oakley, "Supervision Through Videotaping" (June 1991) Paper prepared at Grace Theological Seminary, Winona Lake, IN.

Supervision Techniques

10

Principles for Conferencing with Teachers

So then let us pursue the things which make
for peace and the building up of one another.
(Romans 14:19)

Chapter highlights....

Biblical principles for conferencing
Purposes of conferences
Pre- and post-observation conferences
Dealing with teacher resistance

The story is told of the woman who informed her pastor that she intended to ask her husband for a divorce. The pastor's first response was to inquire, "Do you have grounds?"

"Yes," the woman responded, "we have twelve acres just north of town."

The pastor, somewhat taken aback, said, "Let me ask it this way. Do you have a grudge?"

"No," the woman replied, "but we have a carport."

By now the pastor's frustration was rising, and he tried another approach. "Does your husband beat you up?"

"No," said the woman, "I get up before he does every morning."

Finally, in desperation, the pastor asked bluntly, "Why do you want a divorce?"

The woman responded, "My husband and I have communication problems."

This tale illustrates the misunderstandings that can develop between supervisors and teachers in conferences on issues of instructional improvement. One person thinks he said what he thought he meant, and the other is sure she heard what she thought she heard. Several years ago a teacher was summoned to a conference with his administrator, who intended to inform the teacher that his contract was not being renewed. The administrator, concerned about not upsetting the teacher's emotional equilibrium, couched the dismissal in such gentle terms that the teacher left the conference oblivious of the fact he had just been fired.

The focus of this chapter is on supervisors' conferences with teachers before and after classroom observations. The principles and guidelines, however, apply to a broad range of conference settings.

What Biblical Principles Apply to Conferencing?

Chapter 1 describes biblical principles that relate to supervision. Several of these have particular relevance in the conference setting, and these should guide the motivation, attitude, and demeanor of supervisors as they conference with teacher. Listed below are the Bible references and principles of chapter 1 as they apply to teacher conferencing.

Verses	Biblical Principle	Application
Romans 13:4; 1 Peter 2:14	Those in authority are responsible to feed, take oversight, and be examples.	Administrators guide and nourish teachers during conferences.
Galatians 5:13	Mutual submission calls for mutual service.	Administrators realize that conferencing is actually a service to their subordinates.
Ephesians 6:9	Masters should serve employees, not threaten them.	Administrators use conferences for growth, not judgment.
Ephesians 4:25	Truthfulness in relationships is important.	Administrators are open with teachers about substandard performance.
Galatians 6:1	One who falls should be restored.	Administrators seek in every possible way to assist struggling teachers.

What Is the Purpose of Conferences?

A key purpose of conferences is to build on and increase the trust relationship between supervisors and teachers. This is the goal of pre- and post-observation conferences, as well as of summative, evaluative conferences. To fulfill this purpose, communication must be clear and open. Both the supervisor and the teacher should strive for honesty, not allowing any hidden agenda to hide the truth. A simple diagram known as the "Johari Window" pictures this phenomenon:

	What the Supervisor Knows About the Teacher	What the Supervisor Does Not Know About the Teacher
What the Teacher Knows About Him- or Herself	Open self	Hidden self
What the Teacher Does Not Know About Him- or Herself	Blind self	Undiscovered self

Hidden or Secret Self This quadrant contains information that teachers know about themselves but, for whatever reasons, do not reveal to supervisors. Perhaps they feel insecure, or ashamed of their classroom difficulties, or uncertain of how their supervisors will respond if they admit they have problems. If this quadrant describes the information flow, supervisors must work at building trust in their teachers. Only then will teachers voluntarily disclose data that supervisors must know if the conferences are to result in instructional improvement.

Undiscovered or Subconscious Self Information in this quadrant is hidden to both supervisors and teachers. It exists but is not easily perceived. The information may involve teachers' inner motivations and certain subdued attitudes or values that, unknown to teachers and supervisors alike, are affecting instructional quality. The Christian, of course, understands that the entrance of God's Word gives light and that the Holy Spirit is able to convict and reveal. Thus supervisors and teachers must be regularly in prayer, asking God to show them the thoughts and intents of their hearts. In serious cases, it may be wise to involve a trained Christian counselor, who can help the teacher come to a biblical understanding of herself and her actions.

Blind Self The blind self is akin to the subconscious self except that the supervisor knows the truth about the teacher's classroom performance while the teacher does not. Because of personal insecurity or a blunted perception of reality, teachers may not be willing to admit to themselves that they have problems with their classroom instruction. A good approach is the clinical supervision process (see chapter 5), in which supervision is somewhat collaborative, reducing the threat that teachers may feel if they recognize and admit their deficiencies. Another approach is to collect enough raw data so that the teacher cannot help noticing and acknowledging the truth about what happens in her classroom. Viewing a videotape of her classes will help her see herself as she is.

The Johari Window model suggests that supervisors and teachers should work to get as much information as possible into in the "public or open self" quadrant. By doing so, they will be able to diagnose problems accurately and deal with them effectively. Now, with the Johari Window as a backdrop, we will consider several purposes for conferences.

What Should Pre-Observation Conferences Accomplish?

Conferencing with a teacher prior to a formal classroom observation has merit for several reasons. First, such a conference can establish the supervisor as a thoughtful organizer. Teachers will sense that supervisors are planning ahead and not doing things at the last minute. Naturally, this knowledge builds trust and appreciation in the teacher.

Second, the pre-observation conference should put the teacher at ease about the purposes of the observation. Unless the teacher's contract renewal is in jeopardy and he has been clearly told so, the observation is intended to help him, not judge him. The teacher should not need to fear the consequences of an observation.

Finally, pre-conferences enable teachers to explain what the supervisor will observe, to announce their lesson plans in advance, and to request that the observer note particular areas of classroom dynamics.

Pre-observation conferences are typically short, often ten to fifteen minutes. Supervisors identify the purpose of the observation and explain the procedures to be followed. They should also do the following:
• Let the teacher examine the observation form
• Inform the teacher that the observer will be writing during class
• Schedule the observation for a time when teacher will present a subject for which he needs and wants observer input
• Schedule a post-observation conference for follow-up or data feedback

If working with experienced teachers, supervisors may simply ask, *What specifically would you like me to observe?* Teachers usually can identify at least one teaching area for which they would appreciate a supervisor's input.

In short, the pre-observation conference should be relaxed, friendly, and positive. Supervisors should pray with their teachers, submitting the observations and their results to the lordship of Christ.

What Should Post-Observation Conferences Accomplish?

Post-observation conferences should produce (1) an awareness in teachers of what happened in their class, (2) an analysis of those events, (3) an evaluation of those events, and (4) a plan of action for improvement or problem-solving. In other words, one might ask:
• What happened?
• What did it mean?
• Is it important that the teacher make changes?
• What will the teacher do about it?

These objectives can be met in more than one way. Depending on the teacher's personal and professional maturity, one of several types of conferences may be used. (For focused discussions of supervising various teacher types, see chapters 12–14.)

Basic ingredients of all post-observation conferences   Regardless of the teacher's level of maturity, certain foundational elements should underlie all conferences. First, a *trust relationship* between supervisor and teacher should head off any suspicion about motives. The teacher, secure in the knowledge that the supervisor is concerned for his personal and professional welfare, is truthful. The supervisor, trusting that the teacher is concerned about instructional quality, assumes that he wants to make the improvements indicated. Trust is a two-way street.

Second, all conferences make use of data that describe classroom activities and dynamics truthfully. Without an accurate picture of what happened in the class, both supervisor and teacher must resort to personal impressions, which have their place but lack the power of clear data. It is more helpful for the supervisor to say, *Here's what happened. What do you think was the cause?* than to say, *I think the cause of this student reaction was....*

Third, in all conferences supervisors should aim to let the teachers themselves analyze classroom events, identify underlying causes, and suggest improvements.

When a teacher, guided by the supervisor's gentle questioning, creates solutions to classroom problems, he enhances his ownership of the remedy, and he is more likely to make long-term changes.

Finally, all conferences should end with a plan for action and follow-up. Teachers should leave the discussion equipped with a clear idea of what strategies or methods they will implement in the coming weeks. At the same time, accountability mechanisms should exist so teachers will have an opportunity to report progress and discuss further refinements to their teaching.

How Should Conferences Differ According to Teacher Type?

As noted in chapter 4, teachers differ in what approach to supervision will best suit their level of personal and professional maturity. How their supervisors communicate in conferences should reflect an awareness of these differences. For some teachers, supervisors need to bring much analysis and many ideas to the post-observation conference. For others, the conference is a collaborative effort to arrive at solutions. For professionally mature teachers, conferences are opportunities to explore self-created analyses and ideas with supervisors.

Conference for supervisor-generated analysis This conference type usually takes place with teachers who may not have enough knowledge or experience to determine problem areas. Thus supervisors must be ready to suggest problem areas and offer possible solutions:

Supervisor	Teacher
1. Establishes positive climate by verbal and nonverbal action	1. Feels comfortable enough to talk openly about her teaching
2. Presents classroom observation data	2. Learns what happened in specified areas observed
3. Waits for teacher's comments	3. Thinks about the meaning of the data
4. Asks awareness questions, if necessary, to lead teacher to recognize the problem	4. Talks about observed data and what they mean
5. Asks, What do these data indicate to you?	5. Tells what the data mean—that is, a problem exists; something is amiss
6. Explores the meaning of the data with the teacher, indicating that a problem exists	6. Explores the nature of the problem and possibly suggests solutions
7. If necessary, asks, What are some possible solutions?	7. Suggests actions that may solve the problem

8. Agrees with teacher's suggested solutions and/or gives own possible solutions	8. Explores and agrees to implement possible solutions
9. Sets follow-up observation and conference time	9. Proposes or agrees to follow-up steps, including another observation and conference
10. Ends conference	10. Ends conference

The supervisor enters this kind of conference already aware that classroom problems exist. Although the supervisor may attempt to draw insights and solutions out of the teacher, she must often initiate these insights and solutions. (See chapter 12, "Supervising the Apprentice Teacher.")

Conference for collaborative analysis Other teachers will be able to engage in more collaborative work with supervisors. These teachers may have well-founded ideas about effective teaching, but they may not be putting their ideas into practice. Supervisors must be equipped to ask questions that will make teachers think about what they do and might do in class. The conference could follow this sequence:

Supervisor	Teacher
1. Establishes a positive climate by verbal and nonverbal action	1. Feels comfortable enough to talk openly about his teaching
2. Presents classroom observation data	2. Learns what supervisor saw in areas observed
3. Waits for teacher's comments	3. Thinks about the meaning of the data
4. Asks awareness questions, if necessary, to lead teacher to recognize the problem	4. Talks about observations and what they mean
5. Asks, What do these data indicate to you?	5. Tells what these data mean, how teaching is in line with beliefs, what alternatives exist
6. Explores nature of teaching and what the teacher is doing well; possibly suggests avenues for further development	6. Explores meaning of data with supervisor; may indicate or agree that a problem exists
7. If necessary, asks, What are some alternative ways of teaching? or What avenues for further professional development are open to you?	7. Offers alternative ways of teaching and areas for further professional improvement
8. Gives own suggestions or agrees with the teacher's	8. Explores and agrees with suggested alternatives and new directions
9. Sets follow-up steps	9. Agrees to follow-up steps
10. Ends conference	10. Ends conference

In this conference both the supervisor and the teacher analyze classroom data and suggest growth and improvement strategies. (See chapter 13, "Supervising the Journeyman Teacher.")

Conference for teacher-generated analysis Experienced, professional Christian teachers may only need to be shown what happened during their classroom instruction. They will have the wisdom and insight to analyze classroom events themselves, and they can probe with greater precision than can administrators. A conference with such a teacher might proceed as follows:

Supervisor	Teacher
1. Establishes positive climate by verbal and nonverbal action	1. Feels comfortable enough to talk openly about his or her teaching
2. Presents classroom observation data	2. Learns what supervisor saw in areas observed
3. Waits for teacher's comments	3. Thinks about the meaning of the data
4. Asks awareness questions, if necessary, to elicit teacher's response to data	4. Talks about the data and what they mean
5. Discusses possible follow-up steps	5. Proposes or agrees to next steps
6. Ends conference	6. Ends conference

In this conference, the supervisor does not analyze the information, nor does she prescribe solutions but leaves them for the teacher to suggest. (See chapter 14, "Supervising the Master Teacher.") For conferences to result in the greatest amount of positive change, supervisors need to be sensitive to the right match between the teacher's maturity level and the type of conference.

What Oral Communication Skills Are Helpful in Post-Observation Conferencing?

Supervisors who are sensitive communicators can reduce possible tensions and increase understanding. Some helpful skills include:

Open the conference with clarity and congeniality.	Clearly state the conference purpose. Review objective classroom observation data. Invite discussion continuously.
Use questions.	Were you aware of —? What was the purpose of —? Did this activity happen as you planned? Was this technique successful? What is your evaluation of the lesson?
Stay focused.	Discuss relevant topics and data. Avoid "chasing rabbits."
Contribute but do not dominate.	Report observation data. Offer alternative methods from research and personal expertise. Make recommendations.
Crystallize progress.	Summarize important points. Check for agreement on key ideas. Synthesize the relationship between certain points.
Maintain a supportive attitude.	Encourage and praise the teacher appropriately. Relieve tension by smiling often and laughing appropriately. Look at documents with the teacher. Consider sitting in equal chairs rather than behind your desk.
Summarize and provide closure.	Restate the conference conclusions. Confirm agreement on goals and follow-up plans. Pray with the teacher.

Every supervisor should practice conferencing skills by trying new ideas, experimenting with questioning techniques, soliciting teacher feedback on the value of the conferences, and using other suggestions offered in chapter 6.

How Can Supervisors Deal with Teacher Resistance to Change?

What can supervisors do if teachers fail to enact needed improvements following one or more cycles of conference-observation-conference? Teacher resistance to change may appear in several forms, but two primary ones are (1) unwillingness to concur with the truthfulness of observation data, and (2) disagreement on interpretations of data that might require the teacher to change his classroom behavior. From the supervisor's perspective, there are several possible ways to interpret this resistance: (1) the teacher is genuinely blind to the information (Johari quadrant 1), (2) the teacher is being negatively affected by motivational factors (described in chapter 8), (3) the teacher is not walking with God but is in spiritual rebellion, (4) the teacher/supervisor relationship is not one of trust, or (5) the data do not reflect the reality of the teacher's classroom performance.

Of these possible explanations, which ones can supervisors influence? Certainly they can improve the accuracy of data, if that is the problem. They can work to improve some of the motivational elements that may be impacting teachers. They can take steps to improve mutual trust between themselves and the teachers. They may or may not be able to reduce teacher blindness about classroom performance, although videotaping offers excellent assistance here. The teacher's spiritual rebellion must be dealt with in the heart by the Spirit of God, so, aside from counsel and prayer, supervisors are powerless to effect change in that area.

Supervisors, however, can unwittingly cause teachers to resist their suggestions by making conferences threatening; for example, by:

1. Changing the topic too quickly, short-circuiting any opportunity for the teacher to become comfortable and at ease.
2. Explaining what is wrong too quickly, giving the impression that they are seriously concerned about the teacher's shortcomings.
3. Recommending change too forcefully. Suggestions should not be cast as threats.
4. Quickly approving ideas that agree with their own perceptions; thus the teacher feels compelled to please the supervisor, saying what the supervisor wants to hear rather than offering honest, reflective comments.

Given, then, that supervisors by God's grace can soften teacher resistance, what specific actions can supervisors employ in conferences? The ideas that follow fall into two categories. First, if supervisors want to give teachers the benefit of the doubt and agree that the data may not accurately portray classroom performances, they can offer to improve the data in several ways:

1. **Invite the teacher to collaborate in collecting the data.** The supervisor's initial intent for the conference was to collaborate with the teacher in analyzing and interpreting the data. That purpose being blunted, the supervisor may suggest that the teacher gather data by personal audio- or videotaping, or by asking another teacher to observe a class and take notes. In other words, the supervisor may invite the teacher to collaborate in collecting the data as well as in analyzing and interpreting them.

2. **Schedule another observation.** The supervisor can cordially agree to collect additional data on the teacher. The teacher may claim to have had a bad day because of lack of sleep or headache. If the first observation revealed "off day" teacher behavior, the second observation should reflect the teacher's regular pattern. If the teacher deliberately modifies behavior without admitting it, the supervisor can still take heart that improved classroom performance is indeed possible for that teacher. The new data can become the basis for higher expectations and goal-setting for the teacher.

3. **Suggest an alternate means of collecting data.** This approach is a combination of (1) inviting the teacher to collaborate in collecting the data and (2) scheduling another observation. For example, the supervisor may offer to collect data by another means, such as student feedback forms, videotaping, or asking a peer teacher to observe the classroom. In any case, the goal is to give the teacher every opportunity to ensure that the data are accurate and valid so that he or she can plan and implement effective instructional improvements. Supervisors hope that the data collected will clarify the classroom performance issues so that teachers will agree that the data are accurate, will not offer any resistance, and will activate the needed changes.

The second category of supervisory strategy is appropriate when supervisors are confident that the data are accurate in portraying classroom dynamics. Under this condition, supervisors should employ more direct approaches:

1. **Be firm in one's knowledge.** If supervisors are confident the data are accurate and valid, they should not retreat. Firmness and confidence, without anger, are needed. If the supervisor appears to be irritated, the teacher's resistance to the validity of the data may intensify. Perhaps a second, patient, modified presentation of the data will clarify the teacher's perceptions.

2. **Proceed unilaterally.** With this approach, the supervisor may comment to the teacher that he recognizes the teacher is rejecting the data. Nevertheless, the supervisor accepts the data, explaining his interpretation and describing appropriate changes for the teacher to implement. Basically, the supervisor is "requiring" the teacher to improve.

Chapter Summary

Teacher conferences must exemplify the biblical principles that should govern supervisor-teacher relationships, including the need to practice honesty, gentleness, and restoration, and to avoid the misuse of power.

A primary purpose of conferencing is to increase trust and honesty between the administrator and the teacher. As trust and honesty develop, information about the teacher's classroom behavior becomes more open, making effective improvement plans possible.

Pre-observation conferences should set a supportive tone for classroom visits by supervisors. Teacher input should be solicited, and plans for observation follow-up should be established.

Post-observation conferences will vary in structure and purpose, depending on the teacher's maturity. Supervisors should adapt conference goals to teacher needs. Some teachers can develop their own improvement goals, while others require forthright mandates from supervisors.

If teachers resist conferencing and change, administrators should analyze possible reasons and employ techniques designed to soften their resistance and encourage their cooperation.

Supervisor's Prayer

Dear Father in Heaven, please grant me the patience and humility to be a true servant while conferencing with teachers. Season my speech, as it were, with salt. May I speak the truth in love. May our conferences abound with true fellowship among those who claim your name. May the goals and plans produced by our conferences be reflective of the real truth about classroom activities, and may they produce improved instruction in our school. Thank you for my teachers. Bless them with willing spirits and a desire to grow. For the glory of Jesus' name. Amen.

11

Classroom Observations

As each one has received a special gift, employ it in serving one another, as good stewards of the manifold grace of God.
(1 Peter 4:10)

Chapter highlights....

Purpose of classroom observation
Techniques for successful observation
What to observe during visits
Suggestions for observation forms
Observing biblical integration
Observations—announced or unannounced?
Computer-assisted observation

At the rear of the fifth-grade class sat the school administrator, observing an arithmetic lesson in progress. The teacher stood at the chalkboard explaining how to solve problems that require the addition of fractions. At first, her explanations moved along smoothly, but they soon became disjointed. She slowed her instruction, and finally, while explaining an operation, she drew a mental blank. Her words stopped as she searched frantically for an idea. Then, in a burst of frustration, she turned to the administrator and blurted, "Mr. Wells, I just know I could solve this problem if you weren't here!" Later, she admitted to Mr. Wells that she was so nonplussed by his presence that, at the beginning of class, she had accidentally knocked over a coffee cup on her desk. The hot coffee had spilled into her shoe, but she had continued teaching without saying a word about her uncomfortable dilemma.

Herein lies a major question regarding classroom observations. Does the presence of an observer distort classroom dynamics to such a degree that the data collected are invalid and therefore of minimal help to teachers for improving instruction? This chapter will identify the purposes and uses of classroom observations and suggest ways for supervisors to minimize the liabilities of in-class visits.

What Is the Purpose of Classroom Observations?

Why do supervisors visit teachers' classes? Whatever the reasons, they should not include the following:
1. To provide the board with an evaluation of each teacher's performance
2. To follow a practice that is considered the "professional" thing for supervisors to do
3. To compile a personal file on each teacher's performance
4. To see whether complaints about a teacher are true

Collectively these functions reflect goals that are *external* to teachers. They are designed to meet the objectives of others, usually administrators or boards, rather than to benefit teachers and improve the quality of their instruction. When these external goals become the reasons for classroom observation, schools have strayed from foundational biblical principles governing supervision of subordinates. (See chapter 1.)

In contrast, the motives for classroom observation should flow from the true needs of teachers and students. Servant leadership concepts should guide supervisors, and their classroom observations should be used in collaboration with the teachers as a tool for instructional improvement. Thus, supervisors should not do classroom observation perfunctorily or with the drudgery of a mandated duty. It should not be done *to* teachers but *with* them. The purpose is improved instruction, not the fulfillment of an administrative assignment.

So the bedrock issue is motive. If classroom observations are done for the right reasons, supervisors can employ techniques that minimize the limitations of classroom observation and make them an effective supervisory activity.

How Can the Liabilities of Classroom Observation Be Minimized?

Despite its drawbacks, classroom observation is a staple of supervisory practice, and rightly so. It is the one activity in which supervisors actually view teachers' work firsthand. For that reason, every effort should be made to avoid possible distortions. The following suggestions address three limitations of classroom observation: artificiality, observer bias, and the inability to record everything.

Artificiality The potential for students and teachers to behave artificially during classroom visits is very real. The example mentioned at the beginning of this chapter is one illustration. To minimize the problem, observers should:

1. Remain as unobtrusive as possible while visiting classes. The supervisor should have a full view of the classroom while remaining "in the corner," so that teachers and students soon forget a visitor is present.
2. Conduct frequent observations, or schedule observations on several successive days. The more frequent the visits, the less artificial the behavior of students and teachers will be as they become accustomed to an administrator's presence.
3. Inform teachers in advance that the administrator will be writing during the observation. That knowledge will prevent the teacher from imagining that the observer is recording nothing but teacher errors.
4. Stay through an entire class session. If the observer walks out halfway through the class period, teachers and students may lose focus. An observer who must leave early should notify the teacher in advance.
5. Enter the room before class begins. In this way, questions or greetings from students will not disrupt but will be part of the natural flow of events. Be aware that the age and maturation of students may also influence artificiality. Younger children tend to revert quickly to normal behavior as their awareness of a visitor wanes, while older students remain aware of a visitor's presence and will exercise restraint on their normal classroom behavior.
6. Do not participate in the class activities unless you have previously agreed with the teacher to do so. Drawing attention to one's presence as an observer encourages artificiality. On occasion, teachers will voluntarily draw an observer in with a question or comment, though unfortunately, this reminds students of the supervisor's presence.

Teacher artificiality is a real problem, but it is minimized when secure trust relationships exist between supervisors and teachers. Teachers will normally experience some anxiety when their performance is displayed to anyone other than students. However, they are more likely to conduct classes in a "business as usual" manner if they are secure in the knowledge that the data their supervisor collects will be used to help them improve instruction rather than to determine whether their contract will be renewed.

Supervisors must give special care to assure teachers that their trust is warranted. Honesty and openness are key ingredients. Appropriate pre-conferencing before formal observations helps set a tone of trust, as does allowing teachers to respond directly to student or parent complaints the administrator receives.

Observer bias Another problem with classroom observations is the intrusion of observer bias into the recording and interpretation of behaviors. This problem is compounded because supervisors are not usually aware that personal biases have influenced their findings.

Two primary types of bias can develop. One is *bias originating from a supervisor's preconceptions about the teacher*. Consider the following illustrative scenario: The supervisor has heard rumors that a teacher's class is not orderly or well managed. The supervisor begins a classroom observation with the full expectation of seeing chaos at work. When student behavior during this visit fails to live up to the preconceived bias, the supervisor is relieved and tends to feel that discipline problems are not nearly so severe as reported, producing the evaluation that the teacher is doing well.

In this situation, observer bias has entered the picture. If the same student behavior were demonstrated in the classroom of a teacher known for excellent control, the supervisor might assume the teacher's performance was substandard and should not be commended. Either way, the supervisor's bias has affected the teacher's performance evaluation.

The second type of bias results from the *supervisor's incomplete knowledge of effective teaching approaches*. For example, the supervisor enters each classroom observation with rigid ideas about the methods used by all good teachers. In classroom observations, then, the supervisor compares individual teacher behaviors with those ideas, permitting little leeway and failing to recognize effective teaching methods that do not fit the preconceived mold. Observer bias has created prejudice against the teacher's instructional approach, regardless of whether or not it is effective.

This type of bias often surfaces when supervisors overemphasize certain aspects of the classes they observe. For example, they may notice student talk patterns to the exclusion of teacher management techniques. Or they may concentrate on lesson content and overlook the suitability of instructional delivery for the students' cognitive development level. Such bias often stems from the supervisor's lack of confidence in his own knowledge of effective classroom procedures.

In essence, observer bias can create distorted or unbalanced collections of classroom data that interfere with supervisors' abilities to give genuine professional assistance to teachers. To minimize the problem, supervisors can implement the following antidotes for observer bias.

1. **Supervisor awareness that bias exists** This antidote is foundational because supervisors will not be open to change until they admit they can have slanted views of classroom episodes. Once aware, supervisors should make their biases a subject of diligent prayer concern.

2. **Expanding and deepening supervisor understanding of effective teaching**
   Supervisors should take every professional training opportunity to grow in
   their ability to recognize effective and ineffective teaching. They should
   observe teachers known to be masters of their art. They should study current
   research. They themselves should teach at least one class in which they practice educational ideas to gain firsthand knowledge of successful techniques.

3. **Reducing subjectivity during the actual observation** If supervisors are
   subject to the injection of bias during classroom observations, they should
   use an observation instrument that calls for recording objective data, not
   open-ended, subjective data.

Inability to record everything A third major limitation of classroom observation is that supervisors cannot write down everything that happens in a class.
They can make anecdotal records of classroom events, and they can record fre-
quencies of behaviors on special forms. They can record suggestions that occur
to them as the class progresses. Even so, observers cannot record all pertinent
classroom events. Observations are just samples of the teachers' instructional
behavior and do not provide exhaustive data about their performance.

Because of this limitation, supervisors and teachers must be open to receiving
data about classroom activities through *multiple data sources*, such as *teacher
self-analysis, student-to-teacher feedback, peer coaching, videotaping, and audiotaping.* The use of a number of sources broadens the sampling of teacher and
student behaviors and results in a more reliable evaluation.

Supervisors may also consider doing *multiple observations* of teachers, possibly on
consecutive days. These may involve consecutive observations of the same class
(for example, visiting third-grade science on Tuesday, Wednesday, and Thursday)
or frequent formal and informal visits throughout the year. In 1990, Christian
school administrators reported that they conducted an average of 2.6 formal visits per teacher each year and 4.8 informal visits per teacher each year.[1] An experienced Christian school administrator in Florida made it a daily practice to slip
unobtrusively into the rear of a classroom and spend 10 to 15 minutes reading
his mail while class was in session. Later in the day, he would say a word of
encouragement or suggestion to the teacher as appropriate. Robert Schain suggests that "every teacher should be observed by the supervisor at least once and,
more desirably twice, a year. This is the minimum standard."[2]

Taken in concert, these measures can reduce the inability of classroom
observers to record everything teachers and students do and will provide more
complete pictures of events and nuances in class sessions.

Is There a Better Way Than In-Class Observation?

The question may well be asked, Given the technology available today, is classroom observation the best means of obtaining data on teacher performance? Consider the options: audiotaping records only sound; videotaping permits recording of all sights in camera view and most sounds; and student feedback may be distorted by maturity level or personal bias. The best solution to the data collection problem seems to be employing a variety of methods. However, if supervisory time and expertise are available, and if teachers and administrators enjoy a trust relationship, *frequent classroom observation will best achieve the objectives of classroom data-gathering*. Despite its limitations, classroom observation is probably the "single most valuable tool for the supervisor."[3] Such visits also add a personal ingredient in that supervisors and teachers jointly experience the same classroom dynamics.

What Should Observers Record During Classroom Observations?

Since this book focuses on supervision rather than teaching methods, it is unnecessary to present an exhaustive discussion of effective teaching techniques. That would require volumes. (See chapter 7, "Effective Teaching Practices," for an overview.) It is appropriate, however, to provide a simple outline of the basic ingredients of good lessons. In her book *Supervision for Better Instruction*, Marcia Knoll has succinctly categorized these ingredients in what she calls an "Instructional Delivery Skills Checklist."[4] Observing the full range of categories provided on the checklist is appropriate when teachers and supervisors have not identified in advance specific areas of classroom performance to observe. For example, the checklist (see form 07, also on disk) will be most helpful to a supervisor who is observing a marginal teacher with numerous problem areas, or who is doing an initial observation of a new teacher.

Knoll's checklist is a "focused observation guide" as described by Carl Glickman in that it lists focused questions or areas that observers will note and will comment about. Using a predesigned set of questions, observers can conduct qualitative observations by recording answers to specific questions about teacher behavior and classroom activities.

In addition to observation guides such as Knoll's that cover a cross-section of classroom dynamics, Glickman identifies several categories of instruments for recording data on specific behaviors. These include:

1. **Categorical frequency instruments** These instruments list specific behaviors and phenomena. Observers will simply record the frequency of each behavior or phenomenon. For example, the Classroom Interaction Analysis (form 08, also on disk) identifies various categories of teacher and student talk. It is designed simply to provide a count of behaviors that can then be analyzed for trends and interpretations. It can be used when teachers request feedback on specific behaviors or when supervisors have no preset ideas of problem areas and are simply collecting data for analysis. A review of Student At-Task Behaviors (form 09, also on disk) is a sample of this type of recording instrument. In using this form, observers record the number of students engaged in each activity at selected time intervals, usually every two minutes. Another example of this type of observation instrument is the Classroom Snapshot Observation (form 10, also on disk), on which the observer records teacher and student behaviors that are occurring at timed intervals, as if successive snapshots were taken.

2. **Physical indicator form** This type of instrument usually requires the observer to check yes or no according whether certain physical characteristics are present or absent in the classroom.

3. **Performance indicator form** This form, Lesson Delivery Checklists, is similar to the physical indicator instrument except that it focuses on the presence or absence of certain teacher behaviors. (See form 11, also on disk.)

4. **Visual diagramming** In the absence of videotaping, this instrument calls for the observer to diagram patterns of classroom interaction. Often the observer uses a seating chart and draws lines between individuals when they speak to each other. The purpose is to help teachers become aware of the patterns of verbal interaction in the class. (See page 132 for an example.)

5. **Space utilization chart** This approach suggests that observers draw a floor plan of the classroom and its furniture, then chart the teacher's movement around the room during a class session. It is especially helpful for teachers who have difficulty overcoming a traditional, podium-based style. The sample Physical Indicator Diagram records patterns of teacher movement during a class session. (See page 133 for an example.)

Supervisors may find that focused or behavior-specific observation forms are too restrictive for some purposes. When supervisors use intuition, or personal and professional experience, as guides for classroom observations, they will want to use a less structured recording instrument. There are several classes of these:

1. **Detached open-ended narrative** In this method, supervisors record every person, event, or material that attracts their attention. The purpose is to capture unfolding events. The obvious problem is that it is impossible to record everything that is seen and heard, so observers must constantly scan entire classrooms and decide what is important. This approach is useful mainly for experienced supervisors who are already well versed in classroom dynamics. (See form 12 on disk.)

2. **Participant open-ended observation** Participant open-ended observation occurs when supervisors become functioning parts of a class, assisting in the instruction, helping students with questions, using classroom materials, and talking with teachers and students. The participant observer takes sketchy notes during class time and writes in greater detail after class. This approach is useful primarily for experienced observers. (See form 13 on disk.)

3. **Focused Questionnaire** This form comprises five to eight important questions about the lesson presentation on which the observer wishes to focus. The questions may lead through the steps of a lesson progression, or they may ask about other teacher behaviors. These ready-made questions guide the observer in looking for key activities or features. It is a good tool for the less experienced supervisor. (See form 14, also on disk.)

Form 07
Instructional Skills Checklist

Teacher_____Grade/Subject_____

Observer_____Date_____

(INSTRUCTIONS: Check each skill that the teacher is observed performing.)

Preparing Students for Instruction
____ Establishes climate for learning
____ Gains students' attention
____ States what is to be learned
____ Establishes importance of lesson material

Motivating Students for the Lesson
____ Relates new information to prior student experiences
____ Relates new information to prior student knowledge
____ Uses appropriate cooperative learning techniques to motivate learning

Sequencing Instruction
____ Reviews necessary basic skills
____ Presents concrete before abstract content
____ Uses manipulative and visual approaches in conjunction with oral explanations
____ Develops the lesson from simple to complex
____ Checks at intervals for student understanding
____ Periodically reviews class progress that day
____ Confirms what has been learned that day
____ Uses guided practice when appropriate

Providing Review and Reinforcement
____ Reviews and reinforces learning through guided group work
____ Reviews and reinforces learning through individual seat work
____ Reviews and reinforces learning through homework assignments

Involving Students
____ Permits students to respond and contribute freely
____ Maintains appropriate balance between teacher-centered and
student-centered instruction

Maintaining Appropriate Difficulty Levels
_____ Teaches skills new to the students
_____ Reteaches skills not yet mastered by students

Managing the Classroom Effectively
_____ Plans procedures to minimize class disruptions
_____ Communicates rules and expectations clearly
_____ Shows awareness of student misbehavior and intercepts it at earliest stage
_____ Enforces rules consistently and fairly

Uses Good Questioning Techniques
_____ Asks minimal number of yes/no, lower-level questions
_____ Asks questions that require application, analysis, synthesis, evaluation
_____ Uses appropriate pauses after questioning
_____ Asks questions in such a manner that all students engage in thinking

Using Instructional Aids
_____ Uses instructional aids and materials in ways that contribute directly to lesson effectiveness
_____ Uses instructional aids that address multiple learning modalities

Using Books, Texts, and Other Written Materials
_____ Uses books, texts, and other written materials appropriate to the content of the lesson
_____ Uses books, texts, and other written materials appropriate to the students' level of understanding

Integrating Biblical Truth
_____ Involves students in applying biblical truth to content areas
_____ Uses visual materials (bulletin boards, etc.) to highlight biblical truth in content areas
_____ Proactively plans for and integrates biblical truth into content areas

(This checklist was adapted from _Supervision for Better Instruction_ by Marcia Knoll)

Form 08

Classroom Interaction Analysis
(based on Flanders' Interaction Analysis System)

Name_____ Grade/Subject_____

Observer_____Date_____

(Instructions: Using the codes for "teacher talk," "student talk," and "silence" categories, note the behaviors observed at specified time intervals.)

Teacher Talk ...

1. **Accepts feeling** *Accepts and clarifies an attitude or the feeling tone (positive or negative) of a student in a nonthreatening manner.*
2. **Praises or encourages** *Praises or encourages students; says "um hum" or "go on"; makes tension-releasing jokes.*
3. **Accepts or uses ideas of students** *Acknowledges student talk. Clarifies, builds on, or asks questions based on student ideas.*
4. **Asks questions** *Asks questions about content or procedure, based on teacher ideas, with the intent that a student will answer.*
5. **Lectures** *Offers facts or opinions about content or procedures; expresses own ideas and explanations; cites an authority other than a student.*
6. **Gives directions** *Gives directions, commands, or orders with which a student is expected to comply.*
7. **Criticizes student or justifies authority** *Makes statements intended to change student behavior from unacceptable to acceptable patterns; arbitrarily corrects student answers; bawls someone out; uses extreme self-reference.*

Student Talk ...

8. **Response** *Student talk in response to a teacher contact that structures or limits the situation. Freedom to express own ideas is limited.*
9. **Initiation** *Student initiates or expresses own ideas, either spontaneously or in response to teacher's solicitation.*

Silence ...

10. **Silence** or confusion *Pauses, short periods of silence, and periods of confusion in which communication is difficult to understand.*

Form 09

Student At-Task Behaviors

Teacher _____ Grade/Subject _____

Observer _____ Date _____

Instructions: *At each time interval, record the behavior of each student using the following codes:*

At-Task Behaviors: A = Attentive to teacher or instruction
                          B = Working on individual assignment
                          C = Working on group assignment

Off-Task Behaviors: D = Out of seat
                          E = Talking with neighbors
                          F = Playing or inattentive to instruction

STUDENTS	TIME INTERVALS IN MINUTES										
	3	6	9	12	15	18	21	24	27	30	33
1											
2											
3											
4											
5											
6											
7											
8											
9											
10											
11											
12											
13											
14											
15											
16											
17											
18											
19											
20											

SUMMARY OF BEHAVIORS

	A	B	C	D	E	F	TOTAL
Frequency							
% of total							

Form 10

Classroom "Snapshot" Observation
(from the Stallings Observation System)

NAME_____ GRADE/SUBJECT_____

OBSERVER_____DATE_____

(INSTRUCTIONS: At specified time intervals, check all behaviors present.)

TEACHER INVOLVED IN ...											
Monitoring silent reading											
Monitoring written work											
Reading aloud to students											
Instruction or explanation											
Discussion or review assignments											
Conducting practice drill											
Giving test or quiz											
Classroom management with students											
Organizing—teacher alone											
Social interacting with students											
Providing discipline											
STUDENTS INVOLVED IN ...											
Reading silently											
Written assignments											
Reading aloud											
Receiving instruction or explanations											
Discussion or review											
Practice drill											
Taking test or quiz											
Social interaction											
Being disciplined											
Receiving assignments											
Classroom management procedures											

(Information on the Stallings Observation System can be obtained from Dr. Sandra Simmons, 2606 Spring Boulevard, Eugene, OR 97403 or Dr. Jane Stallings, Texas A&M University, College of Education, College Station, TX 77843.)

Form 11
Lesson Delivery Checklists

NAME_____ GRADE/SUBJECT_____

OBSERVER_____ DATE_____

(INSTRUCTIONS: Record the presence, absence, or irrelevance of each lesson element.)

Direct Teaching Lesson
(based on Madeline Hunter's lesson design)

Lesson Element	Yes-No-N/A	Comments
Anticipatory set		
Statement of objective/purpose		
Input		
Modeling		
Checking for understanding		
Guided practice		
Independent practice		

Cooperative Learning Lesson
(adapted from Glickman's Supervision of Instruction, 1998)

Lesson Element	Yes-No-N/A	Comments
Explanation of academic and social objectives		
Teaching of necessary social skills		
Face-to-face interaction		
Positive interdependence		
Individual accountability		
Group processing		

Example of Visual Diagramming
(from Glickman, *Supervision of Instruction*)

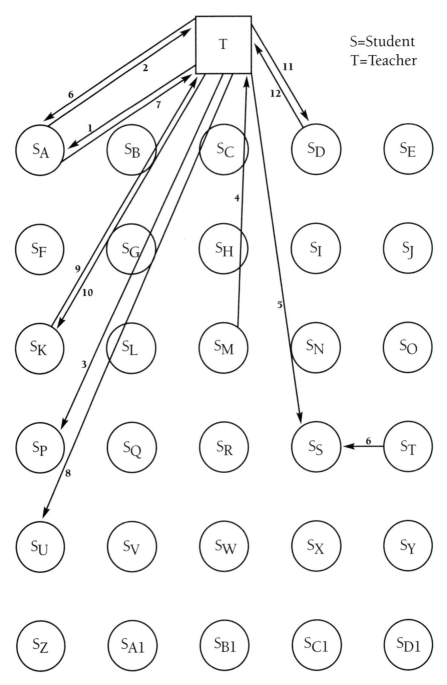

Example of Physical Indicator Diagram
(from Glickman, *Supervision of Instruction*)[5]

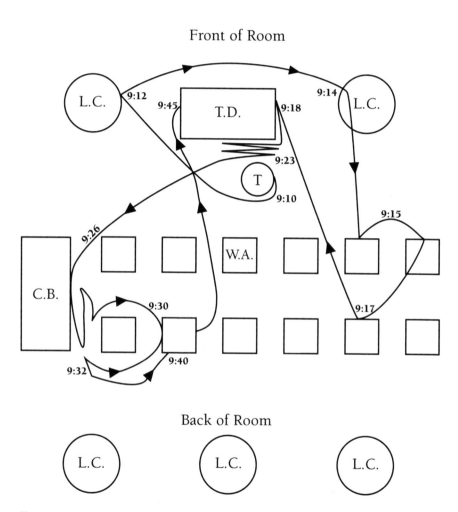

Key:
T.D. = Teacher's Desk
L.C. = Learning Center
C.B. = Chalk Board
W.A. = Work Area

Form 14

Focused Questionnaire Observation Report
For "Direct Instruction Model"

TEACHER_____GRADE/SUBJECT_____

OBSERVER_____DATE_____

What does the teacher do to review the previous learnings that are prerequisites for the lesson? _____
_____
_____
_____

What does the teacher do to present new materials (statement of goals, examples, modeling, checking for understanding)? _____
_____
_____
_____

What does the teacher do to provide guided practice? _____
_____
_____
_____

What does the teacher do to provide feedback for correct and incorrect answers? _____
_____
_____
_____

What does the teacher do to provide independent practice? _____
_____
_____
_____

What does the teacher do to conduct weekly and monthly reviews? _____
_____
_____
_____

(adapted from Glickman, *Supervision of Instruction*)

To determine which type of data to record, administrators should identify, in conference with teachers, the information that will be most useful in meeting teachers' needs for feedback. Teachers will differ on this matter. Some will have specific problems clearly in mind, such as clarity of instruction or attentiveness of students. Others will have no preference for observation emphases and will be content to let supervisors look at all facets of classroom activity. Selection of the recording instrument should match the observation needs.

How Can Classroom Biblical Integration Be Observed?

A key feature of Christian school instruction is the integration of biblical truth into the classroom experience. What indicators enable observers to ascertain how much integration is taking place? The following list suggests evidences of biblical integration that supervisors can look for during their classroom visits:

1. The teacher
   a. Do the teacher's relationships with students reflect a biblical view of the nature of the learner?
   b. Does the teacher conduct instruction according to a biblical view of the nature of learning?
   c. Does the teacher model Spirit-filled conduct?
   d. Does the teacher verbally integrate biblical principles into lessons as appropriate?
   e. Does the teacher give students opportunities to develop connections between biblical truth and subject matter?
2. The students
   a. Do students show evidence that they rely on biblical values in ethical questions?
   b. Do students show evidence that they understand the role of Scripture in the interpretation of scientific theories?
3. The classroom
   a. Do bulletin boards and other wall postings display materials that encourage students to be aware of biblical truth in subject areas?
   b. Do classroom displays include samples of original student work that reveal biblical integration understandings?

These questions form a foundation for observing biblical integration at work in classrooms. They also provide teachers with suggestions for improvement in this area.

Should Observations Be Announced or Unannounced?

There is considerable debate about whether teachers should be told in advance when they will be observed. Some experts claim that observations should be unannounced so that supervisors see classes as they are typically conducted. If they see teachers only in announced, best-performance situations, they may not get data that will help teachers make instructional improvements.

Even those who advocate unannounced visits will admit that it is better with new teachers to announce visits in advance. The stage fright and apprehension that may grip new teachers when administrators enter their classroom unannounced are counterproductive to the purpose of gathering accurate information. Under these conditions, supervision earns its reputation as "snoopervision."

The important question concerning unannounced visits is, What is the administrator's reason for using them? The motive is crucial because the trust relationship with faculty members is easily fractured when the administrator appears to be "sneaking up" on them to catch them doing something wrong. On the other hand, unannounced visits that are recognized features of the total supervision program, clearly intended to give teachers additional truthful data about their work in order to facilitate their professional growth, can actually dissipate teacher anxiety and enhance trust. For the observation to provide the most benefit, a supervisor-teacher conference should always follow the unannounced visit.

A compromise policy is to use announced visits for formal observations in which entire class sessions are observed and unplanned "drop-ins" for short, informal observations. Under such a policy, teachers should understand the purpose and nature of both types of classroom visits. They should fear neither kind since they are confident of that the supervisor's motivation is their professional improvement.

Can Technology Assist with Observation Visits?

Enterprising supervisors can design applications using word processing or database programs that enable them to input data on a laptop computer. Using templates derived from classroom observation forms, they can enter data while observing classes.

A commercial software program produced by the Educational Testing Service in cooperation with the Association for Supervision and Curriculum Development provides forms for observing and evaluating teachers based on Charlotte Danielson's *A Framework for Teaching*. It simplifies the complexities of teaching, giving benchmarks for success. It provides ways for administrators to structure mentoring, peer coaching, or staff development programs.[6]

Chapter Summary

Though classroom observation has its pitfalls, it remains a powerful tool for helping teachers improve instruction. Wise administrators understand the limitations and use judicious techniques for minimizing them, with special attention to maintaining trust relationships between supervisors and teachers.

A variety of observation instruments and approaches are available to use from the recording of frequency of behaviors to the "immersed anthropologist" approach where the supervisor takes part in class and records events through students' eyes. The type of approach to use must be matched with the type of data needed. Supervisors may also make use of computer programs to assist with data recording and report writing.

Supervisor's Prayer

Dear Lord, I humbly recognize the frailty of my flesh in making accurate observations of other human beings. You know my heart, O God, and that my desire is to glorify your name through the supervision process. Please grant me a divine sensitivity to teachers and students in classroom settings. Please give my teachers a peaceful, accepting spirit when classroom observations are scheduled. May Jesus Christ be honored by the manner in which I carry out this aspect of school administration. Amen.

Endnotes

1. Gordon B. Brown, unpublished survey taken at Grace Theological Seminary (Winona Lake, IN, 1990).
2. Robert L. Schain, *Supervising Instruction: What It Is and What How to Do It* (Brooklyn, NY: Educators Practical Press, 1988), 66.
3. *Ibid.*, 64.
4. Marcia Knoll, *Supervision for Better Instruction* (Englewood Cliffs, NJ: 1987), 100–101.
5. Visual diagram examples were adapted from Carl Glickman, *Supervision of Instruction: A Developmental Approach* (1990).
6. *Pathwise Software: A Framework for Teaching* (Princeton, NJ: Educational Testing Service, 1998).

Documents on Disk

Form 07 Instructional Skills Checklist
Form 08 Classroom Interaction Analysis
Form 09 Student At-Task Behaviors
Form 10 Classroom "Snapshot" Observation
Form 11 Lesson Delivery Checklists
Form 12 Narrative Record of Classroom Participation
Form 13 Narrative Record of Classroom Observation
Form 14 Focused Questionnaire Observation Report

12

Supervising the "Apprentice" Teacher

The God of all grace, who called you to His eternal glory in Christ,
will Himself perfect, confirm, strengthen, and establish you.
(1 Peter 5:10)

Chapter highlights....

Apprentice teacher characteristics
Annual supervision plan
Conferencing strategies

T
he administrator was saddened by the news. The fourth-grade teacher, who was just completing his first year of teaching, announced that he needed "time off" from the classroom next year to investigate other career opportunities.

"Isn't there anything we can do to help you change your mind?" probed the administrator.

"I don't think so," replied the teacher. "I have experienced God's blessing on my work this year, but teaching has not come easy. I need to step back from it to evaluate what God wants me to do long-term. I'm not sure I could clearly identify the things that have made this a difficult year."

Why do 20 percent of new teachers leave the profession within their first three years of service? The primary reasons are (1) inadequate preparation and (2) a sink-or-swim approach to their induction. Roughly one-fourth of new teachers lack qualifications for their job, and they typically do not receive the support they deserve.[1] Glickman and Gordon echo these reasons when they describe the inadequate induction of new teachers, including insufficient resources, difficult work assignments, unclear expectations, a sink-or-swim mentality, and reality shock.[2] Early departures from the teaching profession are not confined to the public schools; Christian schools face the same problem.

To address the matter, Christian school administrators must proactively plan supervision and support for their apprentice teachers. In this chapter the author has collected principles and practices from other chapters of this book that relate specifically to apprentice teachers and presented them in a focused discussion.

What Are the Characteristics of Apprentice Teachers?

To understand teachers of all types, administrators need a conceptual framework. Paul Hersey and Ken Blanchard have provided one in their "situational leadership" theory, which classifies subordinates (in this case, teachers) according to maturity levels. *Maturity* is defined as the capacity to set high but attainable goals, the willingness and ability to take responsibility, and the possession of ability, technical knowledge, self-respect, and self-confidence.[3] The resulting maturity-immaturity continuum looks like this:

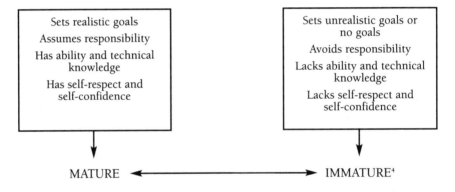

Apprentice teachers may have various combinations of the characteristics on the "immature" end of the continuum. Consider these descriptors of new teachers:

Low skill and knowledge (task) maturity Apprentice teachers need guidance and assistance with a range of skills in order to perform at a satisfactory level. If left unaided, they will struggle to acquire the roles and skills that are crucial to good teaching. They may require mentoring in any or all areas of effective pedagogy, including:

Preparing students to receive instruction
Motivating students to attend to and receive instruction
Sequencing lesson components for maximum learning
Using review and reinforcement during and after the lesson
Involving students actively in the lesson
Strategically adjusting difficulty levels of a lesson
Managing the classroom for maximum attention and participation

Creating diverse ways for students to interact

Using questions in a timely and effective manner

Effectively using instructional aids

Assessing student learning in various ways and in accord with objectives

Integrating biblical knowledge with learning and living.

(See chapter 7 for detailed descriptions of these competencies.)

In addition to skills relating to instruction, apprentice teachers need to master other responsibilities, such as filling out reports, relating to parents, contributing to cohesiveness among faculty and staff, and representing the school to the local community.

Low psychological maturity Some apprentice teachers find it difficult to improve their teaching skills because they lack the emotional readiness necessary to move ahead. They may lack self-confidence about trying new methods or setting realistic improvement goals. Or they may hesitate to tackle time-consuming tasks such as planning and implementing change for fear they will run out of time and energy. Despite their classroom struggles, such teachers find the risks of changing more uncomfortable than the status quo. For whatever reasons, they show an unwillingness to pursue change.

However, many apprentice teachers, though they have low task maturity, demonstrate a willingness to make changes and pursue improvements. In other words, their level of psychological maturity, as related to teaching, is high. These teachers have personal expectations of success and sufficient trust in the Lord to take risks and try new teaching techniques. They show a refreshing eagerness to grow in their ability to deliver quality instruction.

Summary of apprentice teacher classifications Nearly all apprentice teachers lack the ability and knowledge of veteran teachers. Beyond that common ground, they vary in emotional maturity. Some are receptive and eager for improvement, while others are hesitant.

Apprentice Teacher Classifications

Maturity Classification	Task Maturity	Psychological Maturity
Level 1	Lacks the ability and knowledge of a veteran teacher; needs careful assistance and guidance	Sets unrealistic or no goals; lacks the self-confidence or self-respect needed to institute changes
Level 2	Lacks the ability and knowledge of a veteran teacher; needs careful assistance and guidance	Sets attainable goals; has enough self-confidence to make improvements; takes responsibility for improving

How many years of experience characterize apprentice teachers? In most cases, teachers in the first two years of teaching will have some characteristics of apprentice teachers. They will be in the first level of a school's differentiated supervision plan (see chapter 4). After their second year, teachers should have progressed in professional expertise and personal maturity so that, by the end of their fourth year, they can be classed as "journeyman" teachers. Apprentice teachers who fail to grow enough in their first four years to be eligible for reclassification may not be in the right profession. It might be wise for them to consider seeking God's direction for ministry roles that better match their gifts and abilities.

An Annual Supervision Plan for Apprentice Teachers

August—Goal-setting conference For all teachers, at all levels, the year's supervisory cycle begins with a goal-setting conference. This activity is appropriate for apprentice, journeyman, and master teachers alike. (See chapters 3 and 4 for extended discussions, and see the forms Christian School Teacher Job Description and Annual Evaluation, and Teacher Self-Improvement Goals on accompanying disk.) The goals discussed by the teacher and supervisor provide direction and focus for the supervisory activities and the teacher change initiatives.

Apprentice teachers, in particular, may need help in clarifying their improvement goals. First-year teachers may not realize their pedagogical shortcomings until they actually experience classroom realities, and the administrator should be prepared to suggest important goals for them to address, such as the following:
• Clearly identify components of a classroom management plan, including rules, consequences, and rewards.

- Complete weekly lesson plans by Saturday evening before the week they are used. Be sure that each day's lessons are thoughtfully planned to meet learning objectives.
- Anticipate student questions; plan ways to reduce possible confusion.
- Formulate plans for assessing student learning, for grading, for figuring report card grades, and for communicating with students and parents.

These goals are among the crucial ones for first-year teachers. There are others, of course, and effective supervisors work with beginning teachers to tailor goals for each individual.

August—Linking with a mentor teacher Nearly every publication on faculty development recommends that first-year teachers be given mentoring relationships with more experienced peers. (See chapter 9 for a full discussion of mentoring.) Mentors who have the time, concern, and expertise to assist new teachers will eliminate the sink-or-swim syndrome that contributes to teachers' leaving the profession early.

The administrator's role is to identify compatible partners, provide training, extend personal encouragement and resource support, and evaluate the effectiveness of the mentoring activities. If possible, mentors should be journeyman or master teachers who teach grade levels or subjects similar to those of the teachers they mentor.

October—One-week conferencing and observation cycle Apprentice teachers will benefit from intensive, close-up, "clinical" supervision. To provide such support, administrators should plan to devote a full week's cycle to each new or apprentice teacher. Such a week includes a pre-observation conference on Monday, three visits to the classroom on Tuesday through Thursday, and a post-observation conference on Friday. (See chapter 5 for more.) Though it is not necessary that the chief administrator conduct the supervision, the person should be an educational professional with administrative responsibilities (i.e., assistant principal, department head, grade-level coordinator) and the authority to require changed behavior, if necessary.

From this week of supervisory attention, beginning teachers will forge improvement strategies to implement in the succeeding weeks.

One-hour interventions In addition to the planned week of supervision, "one-hour" interventions may be initiated as often as needed throughout the semester to assist the apprentice. (Again, see chapter 5.) These may be done by anyone who is in the assistance pipeline for the new teacher, including the assigned peer mentor, a grade-level coordinator, a department head, an assistant principal, or the chief administrator.

January—Conference to review mentoring progress In January, the apprentice teacher, the peer mentor, and an administrator should meet to review the progress of the mentoring relationship and activities and to set the stage for continued mentoring in the second half of the year. Questions considered at this conference may include:

• In what ways has the mentoring process been positive? How could it be improved?
• How adequate is the time available for mentoring activities?
• How has the new teacher changed and improved as a result of mentoring?
• What areas of teaching should be the next focus of the mentoring activities?

While the review conference is aimed at critical examination of the mentoring process, it should be supportive and encouraging. Each participant should see it as a positive building block in the professional growth of the new teacher.

February—One-week conferencing and observation cycle For apprentice teachers, a second one-week cycle of intensive supervision should take place some time between late January and late March. As in October, a person with administrative authority should conduct this supervision.

May—Summative evaluation Near the end of the school year, an administrator should conduct a summative evaluation (see Chapter 16) of the new teacher's total performance as judged against the contents of the job description (see chapter 3). This evaluation highlights the teacher's areas of strength and those in which improvement is needed. The evaluation also generates improvement ideas that serve as start-of-the-year goals the following school term.

Following the biblically-generated principle that success and continuous improvement are expected, administrators should use the summative evaluation as a developmental tool in the teacher's growth. The evaluation should not be used to judge for contract renewal, unless an intensive assistance (probationary) period has been formally invoked. (See chapter 15 for discussion of "probation.")

May—Final conference to review mentoring progress A final activity in the annual plan for working with apprentice teachers is to bring closure to the year of mentoring. As in January, a conference with the new teacher, the mentor, and an administrator should be convened. The conference may focus on such issues as:

• How satisfying was the mentoring process to both participants?
• How did mentoring result in instructional improvement by the new teacher?
• How could the mentoring process be improved?
• Should the mentoring relationship be continued for a second year?

In sum, the conference aims to identify (1) the impact of the mentoring relationship on the new teacher and (2) ways of improving the mentoring program itself.

Effective supervision of apprentice teachers is critical to their success as Christian school educators. The first and sometimes the second years of service are characterized by intensive supervisory activity aimed at the professional growth of new teachers. The following chart summarizes the activities of this supervisory year:

Time Frame	Activity	Supervisor
August	Goal-setting conference	Chief administrator
August	Linking with a mentor teacher	Mentor teacher
September–October	One-week cycle of conferencing and observations	An administrator
September–May	One-hour interventions as needed	Mentor or administrator
January	Review of mentoring process to date	An administrator
February–March	One-week cycle of conferencing and observations	An administrator
May	Year-end summative evaluation	Chief administrator
May	Evaluation of mentoring process for year	An administrator

What Conferencing Strategies Are Right for Apprentice Teachers?

Supervisors should tailor conferencing strategies to the type of teacher they are meeting with. Some apprentice teachers will be at the "immature" end of the psychological and task maturity continuum. In conferencing with those teachers, supervisors should give careful attention to (1) the teacher's ability to generate effective ideas for instructional improvement, and (2) the teacher's confidence and willingness to try new techniques. The best approach is to let the teacher voice analysis and improvement ideas before stepping in with one's own suggestions. However, not all new teachers have enough experience and knowledge to determine problem areas, so supervisors must be ready to define problems and offer solutions.

Such a conference might consist of the following elements:

Supervisor:	Takes lead to establish a positive climate through supportive verbal and nonverbal means.
Teacher:	Responds by becoming comfortable enough to speak openly about classroom dynamics.
Supervisor:	Presents the classroom observation data for the teacher to review.
Teacher:	Learns what the supervisor saw during the classroom observation.
Supervisor:	Invites the teacher to comment on the observation data.
Teacher:	Thinks about the meaning of the data; comments as able.
Supervisor:	Asks questions about the data, if necessary, to elicit teacher's recognition of problem areas.
Teacher:	Talks about the data and possible problems they may indicate.
Supervisor:	Asks, What do these data indicate to you?
Teacher:	If able, tells what the data mean: a problem exists, something is amiss, etc.
Supervisor:	Identifies problems if teacher is unable to do so. Invites teacher to explore them.
Teacher:	Discusses nature of problems.
Supervisor:	Asks, What are some possible solutions?
Teacher:	If able, offers alternative approaches that may rectify problems.
Supervisor:	If necessary, gives possible solutions and suggests possible action steps to take in classroom.
Teacher:	Discusses possible solutions and agrees to try action steps.
Supervisor:	Summarizes conference, bringing it to an amicable, supportive conclusion. Closing prayer is especially appropriate.

The supervisor enters this type of conference already aware that classroom problems exist. Though the supervisor may attempt to draw insights and solutions out of the teacher, she must often initiate those insights and solutions.

Chapter Summary

Apprentice teachers may lack both knowledge and pedagogical expertise, as well as the self-confidence necessary to initiate improvements. Supervisors should be sensitive to these concerns as they work with new teachers.

It is wise to have a supervision plan for apprentice teachers that contains a good dose of professional and personal support. This support can include peer mentoring, goal-setting, two weeklong cycles of conferencing and observation, and a summative evaluation.

In conferencing with apprentice teachers, supervisors should give every opportunity for teachers to analyze classroom events and suggest improvements. However, supervisors should be prepared to generate solutions and to offer encouraging support.

Supervisor's Prayer

Dear Lord, how grateful I am that you worked patiently with me as a new Christian. Your love and encouragement were most helpful when I didn't know how to behave and, in some instances, didn't have the desire to change. You were so forbearing. Help me to model your principles in my work with beginning teachers. Remind me often of my first days as a teacher. Give me the wisdom to know when my teachers need me to be more proactive in guiding their analysis and growth. In all this, I pray that your image would be formed in these new teachers. In the name of Jesus, Amen.

Endnotes

1. *The New Teacher's Guide to the U.S. Department of Education,* September 1997: cited 29 Dec. 2000: available at <www.ed.gov/pubs/TeachersGuide/teach.html>.
2. Carl Glickman, Stephen Gordon, and Jovita Ross-Gordon, *Supervision of Instruction: A Developmental Approach* (Boston: Allyn and Bacon, 1998), 21–22.
3. Paul Hersey and Kenneth Blanchard, *Management of Organizational Behavior: Utilizing Human Resources* (Englewood Cliffs, NJ: Prentice-Hall, 1982), 151.
4. Wayne Hoy and Cecil Miskel, *Educational Administration: Theory, Research, Practice* (New York: McGraw-Hill, 1991), 293.

13

Supervising the "Journeyman" Teacher

Therefore, my beloved brethren, be steadfast, immovable, always abounding in the work of the Lord, knowing that your toil is not in vain in the Lord.
(1 Corinthians 15:58)

Chapter highlights....

Journeyman teacher characteristics
Annual supervision plan
Conferencing strategies

P rincipal Carlson stared at the ceiling in his office in satisfied, grateful reflection as he thought about the teachers who made up the core of his faculty. Most of them had been hired as first-year teachers several years before, when a tight budget had led the young school to hire inexperienced teachers.

Now these teachers had grown beyond the mistakes and pitfalls of inexperience and had become contributing professionals. How grateful Mr. Carlson was that he had invested intensive supervisory attention in them during their first years of teaching. Now they were capable of coaching each other and mentoring other new teachers. They exuded a refreshing eagerness to serve the Lord, the school, and their students.

Though Principal Carlson's supervisory workload was definitely lighter now, he committed himself to continuing their supervision in a manner appropriate to their experience and needs.

What Are the Characteristics of Journeyman Teachers?

As it did for apprentice teachers, Hersey and Blanchard's "situational leadership" theory provides a conceptual framework for understanding journeyman teachers. These teachers have moved beyond the "immature" qualities, but they are not yet sufficiently mature that they can be released to total self-supervision. They combine characteristics from both ends of the continuum that, taken together, place them somewhere *between* the extremes of maturity and immaturity.

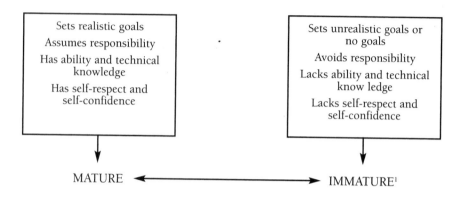

| Sets realistic goals
Assumes responsibility
Has ability and technical knowledge
Has self-respect and self-confidence | | Sets unrealistic goals or no goals
Avoids responsibility
Lacks ability and technical know ledge
Lacks self-respect and self-confidence |

MATURE ⟵—————————⟶ IMMATURE[1]

Moderate skill and knowledge (task) maturity Journeyman teachers have developed a range of pedagogical skills that enable them to perform at a satisfactory level. They no longer struggle to demonstrate the roles and skills that are foundational to good teaching. They understand and carry out good instructional planning, classroom management, student motivation, biblical integration, and assessment of learning. With journeyman teachers, supervisors may spend less energy teaching them how to teach and more time eliciting ideas and improvements from the teachers themselves.

In addition to instructional skills, these teachers understand and represent well the school's mission and culture. They make positive contributions to faculty morale and parent satisfaction. They can be trusted to fulfill non-teaching responsibilities such as preparing reports, attending parent meetings, participating in curriculum development, and others.

Satisfactory psychological maturity Journeyman teachers generally have enough emotional maturity and personal incentive to want to change and improve. Otherwise, they would not have advanced beyond the apprentice level. The danger is that, once having achieved mid-level teaching expertise, they may grow complacent. To address this situation, supervisors should talk with their journeyman teachers about their improvement goals, showing that these teachers are now assumed to be mature, concerned professionals.

Journeyman teachers also benefit from collaborative projects that require the analysis of good teaching and learning: curriculum reviews and accreditation studies, for example. Being involved in such projects motivates teachers to sharpen their own pedagogical processes.[2]

For the most part, journeyman teachers have learned to break through barriers to growth created by low self-confidence, exhaustion, or other personal stressors. However, supervisors still need to be sensitive to potential motivational trouble spots. (See chapter 8 for further discussion on motivation.)

Summary of journeyman teacher classifications Nearly all journeyman teachers have the ability and knowledge to deliver satisfactory instruction. In addition, they have demonstrated good motivation to grow and improve. They can be trusted to engage in beneficial peer coaching relationships and to serve as mentors to apprentice teachers.

How many years have journeyman teachers taught? In the best of cases, teachers achieve journeyman status by the third year of teaching. In all cases, teachers should progress in their professional expertise and personal maturity so they can be classified as journeyman teachers by the end of their fourth teaching year. Unfortunately, some teachers stay at the journeyman level until they leave the profession. Others grow and develop until they qualify as master teachers by their sixth or seventh year of experience.

An Annual Supervision Plan for Journeyman Teachers

The year's supervisory cycle begins with a goal-setting conference, an appropriate activity for teachers at all levels—apprentice, journeyman, and master. (See chapters 3 and 4 for extended discussions and forms to use.) Goals discussed by the teacher and supervisor together provide direction and focus for the year's supervisory activities and for teacher change initiatives.

Journeyman teachers are capable of generating most of their own improvement goals. They generally recognize their own pedagogical shortcomings, and they know how they want to improve. Administrators may need to assist them only in clarifying their improvement goals for the year.

Improvement goals for journeyman teachers are likely to focus on different activities than goals for apprentice teachers. Journeyman teachers are past the survival stage, and they have worked out the kinks of their first years of teaching. Their improvement goals may include the following:
• Refine the classroom management plan to recognize both individual and group behaviors.

- Develop lesson plans that provide for multi-modal teaching that reflects the characteristics of students in the class.
- Refine assessment activities so that, as much as possible, they will capture what students really learned.

August—Agreement to mentor or coach Journeyman teachers are at a professional crossroads regarding peer mentoring and coaching. (See chapter 9 for a full discussion of mentoring and coaching.) They may engage in either mentoring or coaching through several means. They may mentor an apprentice teacher, pair with another journeyman teacher to peer coach, or ask to be mentored by a master teacher. The following table summarizes these options.

Mentoring/Coaching Options for Journeyman Teachers

Function	Partner	Status
Mentoring	Apprentice teacher	The journeyman teacher may volunteer or be asked by an administrator to mentor.
Coaching	Another journeyman teacher	In this activity, peers assist each other, with neither subordinate to the other. Coaching is voluntary but encouraged.
Being mentored	Master teacher	The journeyman teacher may request that a master teacher mentor him or her. This activity is voluntary for both.

The administrator's role in pairing teachers is to choose compatible partners, to provide appropriate training, to extend personal encouragement and resource support, and to evaluate the effectiveness of the mentoring or coaching activities.

October *or* February—One-week conferencing and observation cycle
Journeyman teachers require less intensive "clinical" supervision than do apprentice teachers. Therefore, administrators may plan to give each journeyman teacher only one weeklong cycle per year. As discussed in chapter 5, the week includes a pre-observation conference on Monday, three classroom visits on Tuesday through Thursday, and a post-observation conference on

Friday. The one to conduct this supervision need not be the chief administrator, but the person ought to be an education professional with administrative responsibilities, such as an assistant principal, department head, or grade-level coordinator. Also, the supervisor should have the authority to require changes, if necessary.

One-hour interventions In addition to the formal weeklong supervision, one-hour interventions can be initiated as often as necessary to assist the journeyman. (See chapter 5 for a description of this strategy.) The person to perform these one-hour interventions may be a peer coach or mentor, a grade-level coordinator, a department head, an assistant principal, or the chief administrator.

January—Conference to review mentoring or coaching progress Journeyman teachers who have participated in mentoring or coaching should meet with their partner and an administrator to review the progress of the relationship and activities and to set the stage for continued activities in the second half of the year. Topics to examine include:

- In what ways has the mentoring/coaching been helpful? How can it be improved?
- Is there adequate time for the mentoring/coaching activities?
- How have teachers changed and improved as a result?
- On what areas of teaching should the mentoring/coaching activities focus in the second half of the year?

While its aim is to examine the mentoring or coaching process critically, the conference should be supportive and encouraging. Everyone involved should see it as a positive building block in the professional growth of teachers.

May—Summative evaluation Near the end of the school year, an administrator should conduct a summative evaluation (see chapter 16) of the journeyman teacher's total performance as judged against the contents of the teacher job description. (See chapter 3 for information on job descriptions.) This evaluation highlights the teacher's areas of strength and needed improvement. It also generates improvement ideas that serve as start-of-the-year goals the following term.

Following the biblically generated principle that encourages success and continuous improvement, administrators should use the summative evaluation as a developmental tool in the teacher's growth. The evaluation is not employed to determine contract renewal unless an intensive assistance (probationary) period has been officially invoked. (See chapter 15 for discussion of probation.)

May—Final conference to review mentoring or coaching progress A final activity in the annual plan for working with journeyman teachers is to bring closure to the year of mentoring or coaching. As in January, a conference should be convened with the teacher, an administrator, and the mentor or coach. The conference may focus on such issues as:

- In what ways was the mentoring or coaching satisfying to both participants?
- How did the process result in instructional improvements?
- How could the mentoring or coaching process be improved in the future?
- Should the relationship be continued in the next school year?

In sum, the conference aims to identify the impact of the mentoring or coaching on the teachers involved and some ways the program itself can be upgraded.

Effective supervision of journeyman teachers should not be overlooked, even though administrators trust them to perform well without supervision. There are still ways their instruction can be refined and improved, with the goal that they will eventually become master teachers. The chart summarizes the supervisory year for journeyman teachers:

Time Frame	Activity	Supervisor
August	Goal-setting conference	Chief administrator
August	Linking journeyman teacher with a mentor or peer coach	A master teacher or an administrator
Sept.–Nov. or Feb.–March	One-week cycle of conferencing and observations	An administrator
Sept.–May	One-hour interventions as needed	Coach, mentor, or administrator
January	Review of mentoring or coaching to date	An administrator
May	Year-end summative evaluation	Chief administrator
May	Evaluation of the year's mentoring or coaching process	An administrator

What Conferencing Strategies Are Right for Journeyman Teachers?

Supervisors should tailor their conferencing strategies to the teacher they are meeting with. Since journeyman teachers are likely to be somewhere between "immature" and "mature" on the psychological and task maturity continuum, supervisors should give careful attention to (1) their ability to generate effective instructional improvement ideas and (2) their confidence and willingness to try new techniques. With journeyman teachers, supervisors can relate on a more collaborative basis than is possible with apprentice teachers. The best approach is to give teachers every opportunity to voice their own analysis and improvement ideas before stepping in to make suggestions. If teachers generate their own ideas, they will own them personally, and the changes they make are more likely to be long-term. However, administrators should be prepared to define possible problems and offer solutions, if necessary.

A conference with a journeyman teacher, then, might include the following elements:

Supervisor:	Establishes a positive climate in supportive verbal and nonverbal ways.
Teacher:	Responds by becoming comfortable enough to speak openly about the classroom dynamics.
Supervisor:	Presents the classroom observation data for the teacher to review.
Teacher:	Learns what positive and negative events the supervisor observed.
Supervisor:	Invites the teacher's comments on classroom observation data.
Teacher:	Thinks about the meaning of the data and comments as able.
Supervisor:	Asks questions about the data, if necessary, to enable teacher to recognize any problem areas.
Teacher:	Talks about the data and possible problems, going beyond the administrator's initial questions.
Supervisor:	Asks, What do these data indicate to you?
Teacher:	Will probably tell what the data mean—a problem exists, something is amiss—and will attempt to identify the problem.

Supervisor:	Provides personal insight into the problem; helps clarify it if necessary.
Teacher:	Discusses nature of problems.
Supervisor:	Asks, What are some possible solutions?
Teacher:	Offers and explores alternative actions to rectify problems.
Supervisor:	Responds to the teacher's alternatives, and, if necessary, adds possible solutions and suggests improvements to consider. Invites teacher to propose improvements and action plan.
Teacher:	Proposes improvements and action plan.
Supervisor:	Reaches agreement with teacher. Summarizes conference and brings it to an amicable, supportive conclusion. Closing prayer is appropriate.

The outcome of the conference with the journeyman teacher is a plan of action arrived at through collaborative discussion and joint agreement by the supervisor and teacher. Only rarely will a supervisor have to *require* the teacher to initiate a specific improvement plan.

Chapter Summary

Journeyman teachers have progressed in personal maturity and professional expertise so that often they are able to self-correct. Intensive supervisory attention is not required and, in fact, may discourage professional development if used in an overbearing manner. Supervisors should be sensitive to their journeyman teachers' ability to define their own problems and make their own instructional improvements.

The annual supervision plan for journeyman teachers should be an appropriate mix of occasional clinical supervision by an administrator, self-supervision, and involvement in coaching or mentoring other teachers. When conferencing with journeyman teachers, supervisors should expect them to contribute their own analysis of classroom events and suggestions for improvement that are equal to, and even better than, those the administrator contributes. The results of such conferences will reflect mutual agreement between the administrator and the teacher.

Supervisor's Prayer

Lord, thank you for your patient work to bring your children to spiritual maturity. Thank you also that you give us space to initiate and experiment and, yes, to fail. Now I pray for our journeyman teachers. Please give me the sensitivity and wisdom to continue encouraging them and giving them a reason to strive for excellence. What a blessing it would be for our students if all our teachers had matured into master teachers! With a grateful heart I pray in Jesus' name, Amen.

Endnotes

1. Wayne Hoy and Cecil Miskel, *Educational Administration: Theory, Research, Practice* (New York: McGraw-Hill, 1991), 293.
2. Allan A. Glatthorn, *Differentiated Supervision.* 2d ed. (Alexandria, VA: Association for Supervision and Curriculum Development, 1997), 56–68.

14

Supervising the "Master" Teacher

Who among you is wise and understanding? Let him show it by his good behavior, his deeds done in the gentleness of wisdom."
(James 3:13)

Chapter highlights....

Master teacher characteristics
Annual supervision plan
Conferencing strategies

The school administrator shut the office door, unfolded his portable cot, and lay back in its comfort. He clicked on his CD player and found some soft, gentle music. Next, he took his 5-inch TV from a cabinet, extended the antenna, and began watching an afternoon baseball game. This is the life, he thought. His entire faculty consisted of experienced teachers who were self-motivated, reflective about their work, compassionate yet firm with children, able to deliver positive results, spiritual leaders, and sacrificial in their willingness to mentor and coach each other. He had no worries—no parent complaints, no student complaints, no board member complaints. And all the teachers were supervising themselves!

Then he awoke from his dream!

Of course, it is extremely unlikely that an entire faculty would consist of "master" teachers able to supervise themselves, but that doesn't stop administrators from dreaming of such an ideal. It is more likely that a given faculty will include one and possibly several teachers who are capable of self-supervision. Certainly the way an administrator supervises master teachers must be different from the methods used with apprentice and journeyman teachers. Not only do master teachers require less administrator attention, but they are able to make special contributions to the instructional quality of the school.

What Are the Characteristics of Master Teachers?

Again, Hersey and Blanchard's "situational leadership" theory offers a conceptual framework for understanding master teachers, who have qualities that put them at or near the "mature" end of the immature-to-mature continuum. They are able to set their own realistic improvement goals and to assume responsibility for achieving them. With years of teaching success behind them, they expect to solve any difficulties and find better ways of teaching. They understand that God is the source of their giftedness, and they depend on Him for effectiveness in their teaching ministry.

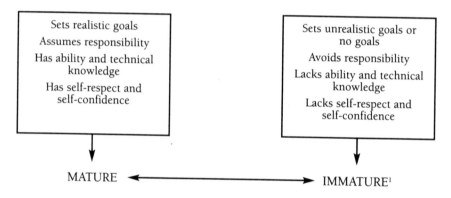

High skill and knowledge (task) maturity Master teachers have developed a range of skills that enable them to be highly effective in the classroom. They no longer struggle with foundational teacher roles and crucial pedagogical skills. They understand and carry out good instructional planning, classroom management, student motivation, biblical integration, and assessment of learning. With master teachers, administrators spend minimal time and energy in direct supervision of classroom instruction. In fact, these teachers probably are more knowledgeable regarding quality instruction, at least in their specialty, than are their administrators.

In addition to instruction-related maturity, these teachers understand the school's mission and represent it well. Even more, they are key shapers of a positive culture and climate. They make strong contributions to faculty morale and parent satisfaction. They are leaders and models. They can be trusted to fulfill all non-teaching responsibilities such as preparing reports, attending parent meetings, participating in curriculum development, and other assigned tasks.

High psychological maturity Master teachers have a personal incentive to change and improve, and that quality has not diminished during their years of experience. However, as with journeyman teachers, it is possible for master teachers to grow complacent at some point. This condition can have several causes—among them, professional boredom. To address this problem, supervisors should involve such teachers in sharing their expertise with less experienced teachers. In doing so, they tap into the adult need to leave behind a legacy.

Master teachers benefit greatly from being trusted with leadership among the faculty. Chairing curriculum reviews and accreditation studies are some of the projects to which master teachers can contribute their expertise.

For the most part, master teachers can participate with administrators in supervisory functions within the school's overall supervision plan. Because they are "at the top of their game," master teachers can expend energy and extend leadership to assist other faculty members in becoming journeyman and even master teachers.

Summary of master teacher classifications Master teachers have proven, by their performance over time, that they can be trusted to set and pursue realistic goals, deliver quality Christian school instruction, and contribute to the professional growth of other teachers. They can be given supervisory responsibilities, thus taking some of the workload off the chief administrator's shoulders.

How many years of experience have master teachers had? In the best of cases, teachers achieve master teacher status as early as the end of their seventh year of teaching. This amount of time allows them to experience classroom dynamics and events in all their breadth and depth.

An Annual Supervision Plan for Master Teachers

August—Goal-setting and professional growth planning conference The year's supervisory cycle for each teacher begins with a goal-setting conference. This activity is appropriate for teachers at all levels—apprentice, journeyman, and master. (See chapters 3 and 4 for extended discussions and forms on disk.) Goals discussed by teacher and supervisor together provide direction and focus for the year's supervisory activities and teacher change initiatives.

Master teachers are capable of generating all or most of their own improvement goals. These teachers are aware of pedagogical refinements or new techniques they wish to develop. Administrators may need to serve only as sounding boards for master teachers as they describe their goals.

During the conference, the administrator and teacher can discuss the role of the intensive one-week supervision cycle, including whether one would still be desirable for the teacher's professional growth. Together, they will decide whether or not to include this activity in this year's supervision plan for the teacher. They will also agree on a professional growth and development plan, one designed to help the teacher reach his self-described improvement goals. The plan will be largely self-monitored by the teacher, with accountability conferences to be held in December and April.

Annual goals for master teachers will focus on different activities than those for apprentice and journeyman teachers. Master teachers are experts capable of modeling good teaching for other teachers and leading them in their own instructional improvement. Therefore, improvement goals can be aimed at the professional contributions master teachers make to other faculty members, the school in general, or the broader arena of Christian school education. Sample improvement goals for these teachers may include the following:

- Work with other grade-level teachers to refine instructional goals and objectives for specific units of instruction
- Serve on an ACSI accreditation team visiting another school
- Chair a subcommittee of the school's accreditation self-study or a curriculum review committee
- Mentor a journeyman teacher who is seeking to extend her mastery of particular teaching skills
- Present an in-service session for faculty or a workshop at a teacher convention
- Pursue additional graduate study, perhaps to earn an additional degree

August—Agreement to mentor or coach Master teachers are at a professional level where they should be expected to mentor and coach peer faculty. (See chapter 9 for more on mentoring and coaching.) These teachers can either mentor an apprentice or journeyman teacher, or they can pair with another master teacher to coach each other. The following table summarizes these options.

Mentoring/Coaching Options for Master Teachers

Function	Partner	Status
Mentoring	Apprentice or journeyman teacher	The master teacher may be expected to mentor a teacher of lesser rank.
Coaching	Another master teacher	In this activity, peers assist each other, with neither subordinate to the other. Participation in coaching is voluntary, though encouraged.

The administrator's role in pairing these teachers is to choose compatible partners, provide appropriate training, extend personal encouragement and resource support, and evaluate the effectiveness of mentoring or coaching activities. Teachers of lower rank must not be given roles that are equal or superior to those of master teachers.

September to May—Optional: One-week conferencing and observation cycle
The intensive, one-week cycle of clinical supervision is unlikely to contribute enough to a master teacher's professional growth to warrant the supervisory time and effort it takes. However, if the one-week cycle is used, it should be with the agreement of the teacher or because school policy that requires at least one episode of intensive supervision for all teachers. Master teachers themselves are quite capable of extending one-week supervision help to other faculty members. They may serve in supervisory positions as grade-level coordinators, department heads, or assistant principals.

One-hour interventions For master teachers, "one-hour" interventions may be activated at the teacher's request. (Again, see chapter 5 for more.) They may be performed by a peer coach, a grade-level coordinator, a department head, an assistant principal, or the chief administrator.

December and April—Conferences to review progress on professional growth plan Since master teachers are trusted with large amounts of self-supervision, occasional accountability conferences with an administrator are appropriate. One conference can be scheduled for December, another for April. The goal is to evaluate the effectiveness of the teacher's professional growth plan.

January—Conference to review mentoring or coaching progress If the master teacher is participating in a mentoring (or coaching) relationship, the administrator should meet with the teacher being mentored and with the mentor (or coach) to review the progress of the relationship and activities, and to set the stage for the partnership to continue during the second half of the year. Several questions may be addressed, including:

- In what ways has the process been positive? How could it be improved?
- Is there adequate time for the mentoring or coaching activities?
- How have teachers changed and improved their instruction as a result of mentoring or coaching?
- On what areas of teaching should the mentoring or coaching activities focus in the second half of the year?

While it is aimed at critical examination of the mentoring or coaching process, the review conference should be supportive and encouraging. Everyone involved should see it as a positive building block in the professional growth of teachers.

May—Summative evaluation Near the end of the school year, the chief administrator should conduct a summative evaluation (see chapter 16) of the master teacher's total performance as judged against the contents of the teacher job description. (See chapter 3 for information on job descriptions.) This evaluation highlights the teacher's strengths and needed improvements. It also generates ideas that can become improvement goals at the start of the following term.

It is possible to save time by combining two conferences. If both the administrator and the teacher agree, the summative evaluation can be merged with the evaluation of the teacher's progress on a professional development plan.

May—Final conference to review mentoring or coaching progress The last activity in the annual plan for working with master teachers is to bring closure to the year of mentoring or coaching. As in January, a conference should be convened with an administrator, the teacher being mentored, and the mentor or coach. The conference will answer such questions as:

- In what ways was the mentoring or coaching process satisfying to both participants?
- How did the process result in instructional improvements?
- How could the process be improved in the future?
- Should the relationship be continued in the next school year?

In sum, the conference aims to identify the impact of the mentoring or coaching on the teachers involved and to define ways of upgrading the program.

Supervision of master teachers should be included in the annual supervision plan, even though administrators trust them to perform well without intensive oversight. Everyone can profit from accountability, and master teachers are no exception. The following chart summarizes the activities of the supervisory year for master teachers.

Time Frame	Activity	Supervisor
August	Goal-setting conference	Chief administrator
August	Linking with a teacher to mentor or to peer coach	An administrator
Sept.–May	One-hour interventions as needed. One-week supervision cycle if both teacher and supervisor agree	Coach or administrator
December	Review of progress with professional improvement plan	Chief administrator
January	Review of mentoring or coaching to date	An administrator
April	Review of progress with professional improvement plan	Chief administrator
May	Year-end summative evaluation	Chief administrator
May	Evaluation of the year's mentoring or coaching	An administrator

For tenured or experienced teachers, many public school systems specify a multi-year evaluation cycle: formative coaching is done for three or four years, and a summative evaluation is made once every fourth or fifth year. In some districts, such teachers are never formally evaluated, but they engage in self-assessment, goal setting, and self-directed professional development.[2]

What Conferencing Strategies Can Be Used with Master Teachers?

Supervisors should tailor conferencing strategies to the type of teacher they are meeting with. Since master teachers are likely to be on the "mature" end of the psychological and task maturity continuum, supervisors should respect their ability to generate effective instructional improvement ideas as well as their confidence and willingness to try new instructional techniques. With master teachers, supervisors can serve as "sounding boards" and questioners. Often the conference will move from specific instructional techniques to more general ideas for the teacher's professional development.

A conference that follows the observation of a master teacher might consist of the following elements:

Supervisor:	Takes lead to establish a positive climate using supportive verbal and nonverbal action.
Teacher:	Responds by becoming comfortable enough to speak openly about the classroom dynamics.
Supervisor:	Presents the classroom observation data for the teacher to review.
Teacher:	Learns what the supervisor observed during the classroom visit.
Supervisor:	Invites the teacher's comments on the classroom observation data.
Teacher:	Thinks about the meaning of the data; comments as appropriate.
Supervisor:	Invites the teacher to interpret the data and define problem areas, if they exist.
Teacher:	Talks about the data and possible problems they may indicate; gives full explanation.
Supervisor:	Provides personal insight into the problems, if appropriate.
Teacher:	Discusses nature of problems, responding to the supervisor's comments.
Supervisor:	Asks, What are some possible solutions?
Teacher:	Suggests alternative actions that may rectify problems.
Supervisor:	Invites teacher to propose improvements to guide changes teacher will make.
Teacher:	Restates improvement ideas along with an action plan.
Supervisor:	For clarity, restates the teacher's solutions; summarizes conference, bringing the meeting to an amicable, supportive conclusion.

Closing prayer is appropriate.

The outcome of the conference with the master teacher is a plan of action largely generated by the teacher. Only in rare situations is the supervisor *not* comfortable with the master teacher's analysis and improvement plan.

Chapter Summary

Master teachers have progressed in personal maturity and professional expertise so that most of the time they are able to self-supervise. Rarely is intensive supervision required. Supervisors should be sensitive to the ability of master teachers to suggest teaching improvements that may be significantly better than those that supervisors can offer.

Master teachers are equipped to assist in the school's overall supervision plan. They can do so through mentoring or coaching, or in official part-time supervisory positions.

The annual supervision plan for master teachers should contain opportunities for both self-development and assisting other teachers.

When conferencing with master teachers, supervisors should allow them to lead in analyzing classroom events and suggesting improvements. The results should reflect mutual agreement between administrator and teacher.

Supervisor's Prayer

Lord, thank you for placing several master teachers on our faculty. They are truly a blessing from you. They contribute so much to the heart of the school and to our students and families. I thank you for their love for children and for you. Please give me the wisdom to know how to encourage and support them and to give them the right opportunities to minister. Give us all the humility to learn from each other. With thanksgiving, in Jesus' name, Amen.

Endnotes

1. Wayne Hoy and Cecil Miskel, *Educational Administration: Theory, Research, Practice* (New York: McGraw-Hill, 1991), 293.
2. Charlotte Danielson, "New Trends in Teacher Evaluation," *Educational Leadership*, February 2001, 14.

15

Working with the Marginal Teacher

*But if any of you lacks wisdom, let him ask of God, who gives to all
liberally and without reproach, and it will be given to him.*
(James 1:5)

Chapter highlights....

Identifying the marginal teacher
Providing intensive assistance
Making a decision

I n the first edition of this book, published nine years ago, the author com-
mented as follows: "Perhaps the topic of evaluating the marginal teacher
deserves a chapter by itself." Here, in this second edition, the topic is
given its well-deserved chapter, underscoring its crucial nature!

Why is this topic critical? The primary reason is that Christian school administrators tend to be as patient as possible with ineffective teachers. If, over a
period of years, a school retains numerous marginal teachers in the hope that
they will eventually improve, the quality of the faculty as a whole suffers.
Public school research suggests that five to fifteen percent of teachers perform
at an incompetent level, but the termination rate is less than one percent.[1]

The topic is also critical because, when administrators or boards finally do
decide to terminate the employment of an ineffective teacher, they often act
precipitously, without having given the teacher any clear warning that contract renewal is in serious jeopardy. The misunderstandings and hurt feelings
that result become part of the school's reputation and testimony, and they can
take considerable time to correct.

From a biblical perspective, two key principles come into play. First, the principle *mandating truthfulness in relationships* requires administrators to be honest with teachers about the quality of their performance. Administrators do

teachers a disservice if they fail to identify and label marginal performance. Second, the principle of *making every possible effort to help* struggling teachers cannot operate if the truth about a teacher's performance is not clearly expressed.

How Does One Determine When a Teacher Is Marginal?

Identifying the marginal or unsatisfactory teacher requires special attention and great wisdom on the part of administrators. It is at this point that administrators often fail to arrive at a clear conviction. Thus neither they nor the teachers involved know for certain when the teacher's performance is unsatisfactory and intervention is necessary.

It is only by performance that a teacher can be identified as unsatisfactory. Since God alone is able to judge the inner person accurately, observable evidence must be the basis for teacher evaluation. This evidence may be observed in a teacher's classroom performance, human relations, attendance and punctuality, adherence to school rules and policies, and personal conduct in work.[2]

Channels for data For Christian school administrators, such evidence will come through documented classroom observations, documented concerns that travel the Matthew 18 or Matthew 5 route, or other observations of teacher behavior, also documented, that have been brought to the teacher's attention for correction. (See chapter 16 for a complete discussion of legitimate sources of data.)

Making the judgment Even when evidence has been compiled, how does the administrator determine whether a teacher is marginal and should be placed on probation? In other words, when has the teacher crossed the line from improvement-oriented supervision to judgment-oriented supervision?

Unfortunately, this decision is always a judgment call on the part of the administrator. There is no clear, easily discernible standard. There is no evaluation form on which ratings can be added up and the teacher who fails to reach a certain score is judged marginal or unsatisfactory. Thus it is all the more important that Christian school administrators supervise their teachers and make decisions about their work in the power of the Holy Spirit rather than simply in the wisdom of the natural mind.

As administrators attempt to determine whether a teacher's performance is marginal, they should consider several indicators:

From classroom observation:
1. Numerous discipline and control difficulties that affect students' learning and Christian growth
2. Instructional and communication difficulties that make learning difficult for students
3. Teacher personality traits ill-suited to working with groups of children

From following Matthew 5 or 18 principles:
1. Numerous complaints that, though some have apparently been resolved, suggest that the teacher is having difficulties
2. Complaints that are not resolved at the lowest level and require the administrator to become involved
3. Complaints that are deep and serious, not trivial and easily corrected

From extra-class observation:
1. The teacher's failure to correct deficiencies when noted
2. The teacher's failure to contribute to the school's unity and mission
3. The teacher's lifestyle problems in violation of the contract or job description

After an administrator has reviewed all the evidence regarding a teacher, the bottom-line questions are these: Have I lost confidence in the teacher? When complaints about the teacher have come, am I afraid they are probably well founded? When the answers are in the affirmative, it is time to place the teacher on probation or impose an "intensive correction period." The teacher is then given notice of the shortcomings and a deadline for correcting them. (See chapter 2 for further discussion of probation.) This decision is never an easy one, and it must be made in a spirit of restoration.

Placing the teacher in an intensive correction period changes the ground rules for classroom observation visits. Up to this point, it has been assumed that the teacher will be successful and the contract will be renewed. Now, however, contract renewal is in jeopardy. Classroom visits, which formerly were made to render assistance, become times of evaluating the teacher's performance for contract purposes. The teacher should be *fully aware* of this new status.

What Is the Nature of Intensive Assistance?

Identifying specific weaknesses and concerns The administrator's first task is to define the performance concerns, the reasons why the teacher is being placed on intensive correction status. These reasons should relate to expectations spelled out in the teacher's job description, the guiding document for teacher performance and evaluation. They should be recorded in writing for the benefit of both the teacher and the school.

Appointing a support and evaluation team The wise administrator draws on the biblical principle that there is wisdom and safety in a multitude of counselors. In the case of the marginal teacher, the "multitude of counselors" may take the form of an officially appointed support and evaluation team assigned to that specific teacher. A marginal teacher needs immediate, effective help that draws on the expertise of more than one person.

This team should consist of three persons whose spiritual integrity, professionalism, and educational judgment are exemplary. The team may include peer teachers, department heads, other administrators, or persons from outside the school such as retired teachers or administrators, or Christian college professors. Each member of the team must be respected, trustworthy, and capable of keeping confidences.

The team's mission is threefold. First, it is to prepare an intensive supervision plan for the marginal teacher. Second, it is to assist that teacher in addressing and overcoming the documented deficiencies. Third, it is to make a contract recommendation to the administrator at the end of the intensive correction period.

Developing an intensive supervision plan After reviewing the administrator's documented concerns about the teacher's performance, the team prepares a 90-day plan of action, including the following elements:
- *Classroom visits:* frequency; whether announced or not; persons to make visits
- *Follow-up conferences:* frequency; persons to conduct conferences
- *45-day progress check conference:* persons to conduct conferences
- *Evidence of satisfactory improvement:* nature of evidence that performance deficiencies have been adequately corrected

An example of such a plan follows, and a blank form appears on the disk.

Form 15

Intensive Correction Plan of Assistance

(sample)

Teacher _____*Jeff Williams*_____ Date_____*Jan 02*_____

Administrator and/or Committee Members

*Principal*_____

*4th-grade teacher*_____

*Retired teacher*_____

Plan for Assistance (conferences, mentoring, classroom visits, etc.)

1. Each person will visit two class sessions and conference with Jeff afterwards.

2. A progress-check conference with Jeff and committee will be held in 45 days.

3. Jeff given 1 day released time to observe senior teacher.

Deficiencies	Evidence Required	Evidence Observed
Classroom control: students do not behave within limits	*Positive reports by committee observers; sampling of comments from students/parents*	
Instruction is not planned and sequenced for good learning	*Detailed lesson plans and weekly plan book; class observations*	

Contract Recommendation

_____ Contract renewal

_____ Contract renewal with continued intensive correction status

_____ Nonrenewal of contract

Administrator's Signature_____ Date_____

If the teacher's classroom performance is the concern, the team may provide various kinds of help, including (1) supervisory help in lesson planning, (2) classroom visits to observe teachers with particular strengths, (3) demonstration lessons, and (4) a "buddy" system with a master teacher serving as mentor.[3]

If the teacher's unsatisfactory performance involves relational problems or other shortcomings outside the classroom, the team should recommend (or require) appropriate counseling, offer suggestions for change from personal experience, or recommend relevant readings. In every situation, praying with the teacher opens the potential for God's power to change the situation.

No effort should be spared in attempting to restore the teacher during the intensive correction period. Above all, it is not a time to cut teachers adrift to fend for themselves.

Considering special evidence Should the support team consult parents or students in order to gather data about the marginal teacher's performance during the intensive correction period? Student feedback has clear liabilities, as described in chapter 9. If the support team determines a need for feedback from students, the teacher should be the one to gather the information and should see the results first, before submitting them to, and discussing them with, the support team. Care must be taken that the Matthew 18 principle is not violated.

The same would be true of any parent feedback. The teacher must request and collect the information. Questions must be worded in a manner that elicits information from parents' firsthand experience, not rehashes of rumors that students bring home.

Great caution must be taken if feedback about the marginal teacher is requested from other persons. The very act of gathering the information can unnecessarily arouse suspicion and draw unfavorable attention to the teacher.

How Is a Final Decision Reached?

Concluding the work of the special support team After support team members have supervised and evaluated the marginal teacher for the 90-day period, they prayerfully examine the evidence they have collected. They arrive at a judgment as to whether or not the evidence demonstrates that performance deficiencies have been satisfactorily corrected. Together they formulate a recommendation to the administrator in one of three categories:

• Deficiencies satisfied; contract renewal recommended
• Deficiencies not satisfied; contract renewal not recommended
• Deficiencies satisfied, but not demonstrated; long-term contract renewal recommended with intensive correction period extended into the next school year

Formulating the administrative decision The special support team serves as an assistance and advisory group for the administrator. Since it is not intended to function as an authoritative body, the administrator must make decisions and take action unless a board of trustees is the final hiring and discharge authority. In either case, the administrator must decide whether (1) to agree with the support team and carry out its recommendation, or (2) to disagree with the team and take a different action. This choice can be difficult for an administrator. It was the administrator who put the teacher on intensive correction status, and it is the administrator who must now come to a decision about what will follow. Again, it is good to remember that God has provided wisdom and safety in "the multitude of counselors."

The "one-incident" unsatisfactory teacher While most instances of unsatisfactory performance are documented over a period of time, there are occasions where one incident justifies an immediate "unsatisfactory" rating. Occasionally, a teacher will display emotional imbalance, sometimes even physically mishandling a student. When such an event is so critical as to endanger the health, safety, or welfare of students, the supervisor must take immediate steps to remove the teacher from the school. The teacher must be replaced until all facts can be collected and a fair judgment rendered.

In Christian schools, critical incidents affecting the school's testimony or the students' spiritual growth may require the removal of a teacher: for example, a teacher uses profanity or other language out of character with the school's teachings, or commits a crime, or is involved in immoral relationships, or teaches heresy. In many Christian schools, such behavior violates contract stipulations, and it is not easily correctable during a probationary period. To protect the school's testimony and the students' spiritual welfare, the teacher must be removed from the classroom until the administrator and board can evaluate all the data and make a decision regarding the teacher's long-term status.

Chapter Summary

Identifying the marginal or unsatisfactory teacher requires special administrative wisdom and attention. Administrators must receive data about the teacher's work from various channels. They must evaluate the data and determine whether the teacher's contract renewal has been jeopardized.

After making the decision to place a marginal teacher on "intensive correction" status, the administrator should appoint a support and evaluation team to work closely with the teacher for 90 days. The team prepares and monitors a special assistance plan designed to help the teacher correct deficiencies, and evaluates the teacher's performance against job description standards.

The team concludes its work by recommending contract renewal, nonrenewal, or conditional renewal. It is then up to the administrator to agree with or change the recommendation.

Supervisor's Prayer

Dear Lord, how my heart aches for the struggling teacher! The person came to our school with such high ideals and hopes of being successful. Now it seems as if teaching may not be her calling at all. I ask you in this special circumstance to grant this teacher special encouragement and vision. May she genuinely experience your care and grace. Please give me, and others who work with her, your insight and wisdom. It is our first desire to see her teaching ministry blossom. However, through it all we will trust you for the proper guidance and results. In Jesus' name, Amen.

Endnotes

1. E. M. Bridges, *The Incompetent Teacher: Managerial Responses* (Washington, DC: Palmer Press, 1992).
2. Robert L. Schain, *Supervising Instruction: What It Is and How to Do It* (Brooklyn: Educators Practical Press, 1988), 144.
3. Ibid., 147.

Materials on Disk

Form 15 Intensive Correction Plan of Assistance

16

Annual Teacher Evaluations

For in the way you judge, you will be judged; and by your standard of measure, it shall be measured to you.
(Matthew 7:2)

Chapter highlights....

Purpose of annual evaluations
Relation to job description
Qualities being evaluated
Sources of data for evaluation

The topic of annual evaluations is actually redundant in schools where administrators practice thorough supervision throughout the school year. When administrators and teachers are both consistently aware of performance progress, a "summative" evaluation can be extracted at any time from what has already been recorded, and its conclusions will surprise no one.

However, some Christian school leaders approach annual evaluation time without any consistent, yearlong preparation. When they must evaluate teachers in the spring for contract renewal purposes, they resort to two days of sequestered meditation regarding the teachers' strengths and weaknesses. They mull over classroom observation data, personal impressions of teachers as contributing faculty members, and the sum total of parent and student comments. From these, they seek to forge a meaningful picture of each teacher's value to the school. What a surprise to the teacher when the administrator announces that the teacher's performance has been unsatisfactory and recommends that the contract not be renewed!

"My brethren, these things ought not so to be." Administrators should construct annual evaluations with foresight, due process, adherence to biblical principles, and much love and concern for the teachers. Evaluations should flow from on-going yearlong supervision. This chapter deals with preparing annual evaluations that reflect these features.

What Should Annual Evaluations Accomplish?

The annual evaluation should resemble a single photograph that captures the truth about the teacher and the teacher's performance. It is a component of the yearlong supervision process. It summarizes the product of yearlong formative supervision. It does not suddenly reveal new information about teachers that was previously hidden or unknown. Annual evaluations also provide opportunity for teachers to reflect on their total ministry. By providing a review of the past and a record of improvement plans, annual evaluations enrich the total supervisory process.

The past: total annual performance The annual evaluation is meant to describe teachers' total job performance against a standard of excellence. It gives teachers and supervisors a broad look at all aspects of teachers' work. It describes the sum total of a teacher's worth to the school. Such evaluations are usually labeled as "formal" or "summative" evaluations.

The future: improvement goals Annual evaluations also provide feedback to teachers regarding their strengths and weaknesses, including classroom teaching. This feedback should be the springboard for improvement goals developed by teachers, either alone or in collaboration with supervisors. Good administrators will blend both teacher and supervisor feedback in arriving at conclusions about teacher performance.

While it is traditional to assume that summative evaluations automatically lead to decisions about contract renewal, in reality they should simply be summaries of assistance-oriented evaluation. They should synthesize yearlong formative supervision efforts into statements about teachers' annual contributions to the school. They should *not* be used in determining contract renewal unless teachers are already in an intensive correction period (probation) and know that their contract renewal is in jeopardy.

Who should conduct annual teacher evaluations? Should it be the same person who visits the teachers' classrooms with the primary purpose of helping them improve? Are teachers willing to trust that person to judge them as well? In larger schools it is possible to assign the annual evaluation to someone else, but in most medium and small schools, administrators must both supervise for instructional improvement and evaluate for contract renewal. As one might expect, it can be difficult for one person to be effective in both roles.

Can a person do a credible job of combining these functions? The answer is yes. As Carl Glickman reports, "It can be done, but with difficulty and only by an individual who can maintain a relationship of trust and credibility with teachers. Ask yourself: Is there someone you would trust to evaluate you for contract renewal purposes as well as to assist you with your own professional improvement? Could you let your hair down with this person? There probably is someone, but it must be a very special person. Only if you believe that the person is primarily concerned with helping you will you be comfortable, receptive, and willing to reveal your areas of greatest need."[1] Certainly administrators who are indwelt by God's Holy Spirit have a supernatural resource for this task.

But what if the administrator is not yet skilled enough to perform both formative and summative evaluation for teachers? The best interim solution is to use other strategies for making formative evaluations for instructional improvement. Among the possibilities are conducting teamwork supervision with a peer teacher, videotaping followed by teacher self-review, or assigning a master teacher to provide instructional guidance. Administrators may then concentrate on summative evaluations. (Note: Administrator skill development is also discussed in Chapter 6.)

How Are Evaluations Related to Job Descriptions?

As noted in chapter 3, the job description forms an essential base for the duties and expectations for teachers. It sets the standard for teachers' performance and guides administrators' evaluations.

If written with forethought, the job description can also serve as the annual evaluation instrument. (See form 02 on disk.) Thus the evaluator rates the teacher's performance against the tasks and expectations it describes, and a separate annual evaluation form is not needed.

What Should Be Evaluated?

When considering what school personnel want evaluation forms to reveal, an important concern is the type of rating that the supervisor assigns to teachers. Three general categories of ratings may be used—*comparative, frequency,* or *criterion-referenced*. Each type serves distinct purposes.

Comparative ratings These ratings require supervisors to compare individual teachers with a certain population of teachers. The rating values often used are *Excellent, Above Average* or *Good, Average, Below Average* or *Fair, Poor*, and *Unsatisfactory*, or similar ones. What do these ratings reveal about a teacher's performance? Unfortunately, they indicate nothing more than a comparison with an imaginary group of Christian school teachers or an imaginary standard of acceptable performance that exists in the mind of the supervisor. Within the population of teachers, some will unavoidably be above average, average, and below average. A comparative scale does not indicate whether the teacher's performance is acceptable or unacceptable in a particular school, and thus it provides no clear basis for determining the teacher's total worth to the school's ministry.

Frequency ratings Frequency ratings call for descriptions of teacher performance that assign a quantitative rating to each behavior. These schemes provide such classifications as *Always, Usually, Seldom,* or *Never,* or similar ones. Another form is *Consistently, Occasionally*, and *Seldom*. While these ratings force analysis of observable behaviors rather than a nebulous comparison with a population of teachers, they do not identify levels of satisfactory or unsatisfactory performance. For some behaviors, it is quite satisfactory to demonstrate them *occasionally*, while other behaviors are only satisfactory when practiced *consistently*.

Criterion-referenced ratings These ratings compare teacher performance against a standard of excellence that all teachers should strive for and can achieve. This type of scheme usually includes words like *Acceptable* or *Competent, Satisfactory, Needs Improvement, Unacceptable*, and *Unsatisfactory*. These words suggest that performance criteria for teachers are not dependent on comparisons between them. Potentially, *every* teacher can achieve excellence. An alternative expression of the criterion-referenced approach is to use a narrative evaluation of teacher performance. This forces administrators to assess teacher behavior without reference to categories or other teachers. Teachers must be evaluated against standards of performance expected by the school. (See form 16 "Administrator's Summative Report" that follows, also on disk.)

Form 16

Administrator's Summative Report

Teacher_____Grade/Subject_____

Administrator_____Date_____

(NOTE: The following report is a summation of the teacher's effectiveness. Written in narrative form, it is an outcome of the formative evaluations already performed.)

Christian philosophy and goals
Personal Christian character and practice
Staff and parent relations
Professional characteristics
Planning
Lesson preparation and delivery
Assessment of students
Classroom management
Additional comments

Contract Recommendation

_____ I recommend this teacher for continued employment.

_____ I recommend this teacher be placed on probation for 90 days.

_____ I do not recommend this teacher, who has been on probation, for continued employment.

Administrator _____ Date_____

Teacher* _____ Date_____

Signature of teacher means he or she has seen the report.

Regardless of which evaluation scheme the school selects, the summative form should flow from the content of the teacher's job description.

What is the biblical mode of evaluation? Imagine a scenario in which Jesus Christ is the school administrator. He would evaluate each teacher as an individual, not expecting all teachers to be alike or at similar stages of maturity and expertise. His evaluations would not be comparative, telling some teachers they are "above average" and others they are "below average." Instead, all teachers would be held accountable for instructions and commands given in the Scriptures. All teachers would be expected to make regular progress. All teachers would be evaluated by comparing their present performance with their past performance; in other words, how much have they improved? Christ would take into consideration the skills, training, experience, and talents that teachers bring to their tasks. "To whom much is given, of him shall much be required" would apply. Jesus' teaching in the parable of the talents illustrates this evaluative philosophy. In that parable, servants were evaluated in relation to the resources they were given, not by comparing their production with that of others.

However, what would Jesus do if certain teachers made good progress, but it was painfully obvious that they were ill-suited to teaching and that their performance, though improved, was less than satisfactory? Most likely, Christ would gently reassign such teachers to ministries for which they were gifted. The unsuccessful term as a classroom teacher was permitted for reasons known only to God, perhaps to deepen or chasten the teacher spiritually or perhaps to stretch the administrator's grace and patience.

What Are Legitimate Data Sources for Evaluations?

Literature on education offers little help in defining legitimate sources of data on teacher performance other than to assert the importance of documenting observable facts. But for biblical reasons Christian school administrators must be especially sensitive in determining which data sources they will recognize for purposes of evaluating teacher performance. Much information that comes to administrators' attention may simply be rumor or half truth. Furthermore, even if it is true, it may not have come through biblically mandated processes for resolving offenses between persons. For example, a parent may complain directly to the administrator about a teacher's performance without ever having discussed the problem with the teacher. Because of such concerns, administrators should consider four data sources as legitimate according to biblical guidelines.

Data the administrator observes The administrator observes the teacher in formal and informal classroom visits as well as in the school corridors, the faculty lounge, on the playground, or in faculty meetings. The administrator also sees written data, including reports, lesson plans, and/or other documents completed by the teacher.

Data the teacher reveals or corroborates If teachers report information about their own performance, biblical processes are not violated. Teachers may also corroborate another person's report about their behavior.

Data that result from following the Matthew 18 principle Matthew 18 calls for resolving differences between people at the most personal and least public level, a practice that minimizes the opportunity for the dissemination of incorrect information, gossip, or rumor. The offending person is given an opportunity to correct the problem with only the offended party present. An issue settled in that way never becomes part of the data the administrator uses in evaluating the teacher.

If a matter cannot be resolved at that lowest level, the administrator becomes involved. The biblical purpose for this procedure is apparently to bring objectivity into the discussion. Information surrounding the issue then becomes part of the administrator's legitimate knowledge about the teacher. If the teacher is proven right and the parent or student wrong, the administrator should not evaluate the teacher negatively just because a complaint reached the third-party level.

If problems involving the same teacher are brought to the third-party level *more than once*, the administrator may want to counsel the teacher about relationship skills even if the teacher is again proven right. While the teacher may have been blameless on the issues under evaluation, the fact that he or she could not resolve the problem without administrator assistance may indicate a difficulty in maintaining effective relationships, an important part of a teacher's job. At this point, the administrator may decide to work closely with the teacher to develop parent and student relationship skills. However, it is legitimate to include the teacher's lack of relationship skills in the summative evaluation, since the administrator became involved while biblical processes were being followed.

Data that result from following the Matthew 5 principle When parents or teachers bring their complaints about teachers to administrators without following Matthew 18, the Matthew 5 principle proves valuable. For a variety of reasons, some parents are timid about confronting teachers directly. They prefer to discuss their concerns with a third party, usually the administrator. First, the administrator should encourage the parents to speak directly with the teacher. Many parents, however, still shy away from that type of conference. In such situations, administrators may consider asking teachers to use the Matthew 5:23–24 principle: "If you ... remember that your brother has something against you ... first go and be reconciled to your brother...." Administrators should lovingly inform teachers of parent complaints and urge them to follow Matthew 5 by going to the offended parent or student, thus addressing the problem at the most personal and least public level. If the problem is not resolved at that lowest level, the teacher and administrator should meet with the offended party. Again, information about the teacher's behavior becomes a legitimate part of the supervisor's data on the teacher's performance.

A special challenge faced by administrators is to avoid forming judgments about teachers before receiving data through legitimate processes. Administrators should do everything possible in a parent conference to prevent parents from reporting negative concerns about a teacher before discussing those concerns with the teacher. When parents report their concerns about a teacher, administrators cannot easily erase that from their minds. How can they head off premature discussions of teacher weaknesses? Very early in the parent conference, the administrator should find out the general nature of the requested appointment. Sensing that the parent is going to complain about a teacher, the administrator may say one of the following:

• Is the teacher aware of your concerns?
• Have you had opportunity to discuss your concerns directly with the teacher?
• Are you aware of the principles our school seeks to follow in situations like this?
• Would you do me a personal favor and set up an appointment to discuss this first with the teacher?
• Would you like for me to arrange a conference for you with the teacher?

These and other questions provide opportunities for administrators to share with parents the principles from Matthew 18, which the school supports and encourages both students and teachers to use. Administrators should make every effort to provoke parents' support and adherence to Matthew 18 *before* they have opened their bag of complaints and spilled them all over the administrator's memory.

Chapter Summary

Annual evaluations should provide a summation of teachers' total job performance while serving as a springboard for improvement plans. These evaluations should be one ingredient of a total supervision plan. Evaluation criteria should flow from the teacher job description and should indicate whether teachers are performing up to an expected standard.

Evaluation rating schemes may be comparative, frequency-referenced, or criterion-referenced. The scheme selected by a school should (1) minimize the subjectivity of administrators, (2) concentrate on observable, documented behaviors, and (3) flow from biblical principles of supervision.

In assembling annual evaluations, administrators must consider only data that come through legitimate, biblical processes, special care being taken to follow the Matthew 5 and 18 principles.

Supervisor's Prayer

Gracious Father, I confess my human inadequacy for evaluating teachers with perfect righteousness and justice. But I thank you that you, as the eternal, holy judge, know the whole truth about every teacher's motives, attitudes, and behaviors. Please grant me a full portion of your Spirit and your wisdom in carrying out the evaluation task that you have given me as a school administrator. I so desperately need it! To you alone belongs the praise for the fair administration of this school. In Jesus' righteous name, Amen.

Endnotes

1. Carl D. Glickman, *Supervision of Instruction: A Developmental Approach.* 2d ed. (Boston: Allyn and Bacon, 1990), 298.

Materials on Disk

Form 02 Christian School Teacher Job Description and Annual Evaluation
Form 16 Administrator's Summative Report

17

Group Techniques in Supervision

And having summoned His twelve disciples, He gave them authority. . . .
These twelve Jesus sent out after instructing them....
(Matthew 10:1, 5)

Chapter highlights....

Research on in-service programs
Guiding principles
Using a needs assessment
Using faculty meetings
Injecting variety into staff development
Planning details

D o the faculty meetings in Christian schools serve to enrich classroom teaching, or are they irrelevant, humdrum sessions that teachers must grudgingly endure? Do administrators run dry of ideas for creative group training? Do after-school meetings cause resentment by increasing the time demands on busy, tired, over-committed teachers?

In-service faculty meetings, which often fit these stereotypes, can actually be lively and helpful. In fact, group staff development sessions offer kinds of training that one-on-one supervision can simply not accomplish. Such sessions can be professionally provocative, inspirational, instructional, creative, idea-generating, and encouraging.

Group approaches to instructional supervision also provide administrators with alternatives to steady diets of classroom observation. They are especially valuable tools for encouraging professional improvement in schools where administrators are unavailable for class observation during the school day.

In this chapter the terms *group supervision*, *in-service education*, and *staff development* are used interchangeably. The focus will be on principles and practices of successful, effective in-service group supervision.

Do Biblical Principles Apply to Staff Development?

The foundation for all practices in Christian schools is the written Word of God. Therefore, in-service training activities should be rooted in biblical principles.

A good starting point for administrators preparing staff development programs is to be sensitive to their human resources—teachers. Administrators should plan programs that are teacher-centered, avoiding the temptation to hold sessions on topics *they alone* believe are needed. They must also resist simply presenting information and naively assuming that they have discharged their responsibility for staff improvement. Instead, they should seek to discover what topics would best meet teachers' needs and would result in actual instructional growth.

Good in-service programs reflect Jesus' approach to discipling. Consider the following features of Jesus' discipleship program:

Feature 1: Training is based on learning needs. Jesus was a master at discerning what His disciples needed to learn. His instruction was designed to fill their gaps in knowledge and understanding, so He focused directly on deficiencies rather than on lessons that the disciples had already learned well.

Feature 2: Training often flows from current experiences. From Peter's walking on water to the disciples' wondering where to get food for five thousand, Jesus took advantage of current perplexities to teach new truths or to reinforce lessons previously taught.

Feature 3: Training is continuous, not once for all time. Jesus never stopped teaching and molding His followers. From day to day, while walking or eating, in early morning or in the evening, Jesus' training continued. He never considered one lesson to be enough.

Feature 4: Training includes practical experience and follow-up. This principle is clearly illustrated in Jesus' sending out of the seventy-two to minister in His name. After they had completed their ministry, the disciples returned to Jesus to discuss their field experiences. Undoubtedly, there was much opportunity to give attention to individual learning.

Feature 5: Training is built around a master plan with master objectives.
Throughout Jesus' ministry, His instruction to His disciples was efficient, effective, focused, and purposeful. He taught as one with a goal, not as one who is uncertain about where the instruction will lead.

Feature 6: Training activity involves the leader. Often Jesus had an integral part in the activities that His training program comprised.

Biblical principles like these bear a striking resemblance to suggestions arising from research on staff development programs. With a biblical foundation in place, administrators can construct a superstructure for in-service training that employs the best of research findings.

What Does Research Suggest About In-Service Programs?

A good starting point in this discussion is an overview of research regarding effective in-service programs. This research sought to isolate components of successful in-service training schemes.

Research Studies In 1978, the Rand Corporation conducted a study under contract to the federal government. Researchers surveyed 852 administrators and 689 teachers. Initially, the company conducted observations of projects on site. Two years later they resurveyed 100 innovative projects that had gone beyond the period for which they were funded. With the resulting data, researchers found that successful projects had several common characteristics, including teacher involvement in planning, practical training, individual teacher follow-up, and administrator participation.[1] In 1980 and 1981, Humphries studied the curriculum innovations of Georgia schools, learning that collaborative planning of in-service activities was significantly related to their success.[2] In a 1974 research review, Lawrence synthesized 97 studies of in-service programs, identifying effective and less effective programs.[3] The findings on effective programs were similar to those of the Rand study.

A study conducted by Joyce and Showers identified the more successful in-service programs as those that accompany group presentations with follow-up and consultation for individual teachers. In 1980, Stallings concluded that small-group problem-solving workshops in which six to seven teachers share and experiment are more effective than large-group workshops.[4]

Mohlman compared three different in-service models and found that teachers acquired more classroom skills when the program included presentation, demonstration, practice, and feedback followed by peer observation. The second most effective model was similar to the first in all respects except that coaching by a trainer was substituted for peer observation. The least effective of the three models contained all the elements of the others but lacked either peer observation or trainer coaching.[5]

Working in cooperative groups is valuable for teachers as well as school-age students. In 1987 Johnson and Johnson reported that collegial adult groups have been shown to produce higher adult achievement and performance than individual and competitive learning methods.[6]

Synthesis of Research Findings Combining the important results of these studies has resulted in a list of features of effective in-service programs. Good staff development plans include:
1. Involvement of teachers in the planning
2. Long-term, rather than short-term, quick-fix planning
3. Released time for teachers
4. Concrete, specific training
5. Small-group workshops
6. Peer observations and feedback
7. Demonstration, trials, and feedback in workshops
8. Regular teacher meetings for problem solving, experimentation, and alterations
9. Participation of administrators and supervisors in activities[7]

A noteworthy point is that staff development programs, though group-oriented, are more effective in producing changed teacher behavior when there is an individualized attention component.

What Principles Should Guide Group Supervision?

By building on the foundation of biblical principles for group training and adding to it the contributions of research, Christian school administrators can develop in-service programs with a strong confidence that God will bless and that improved instruction will result.

Principle 1: Develop a comprehensive, yearlong (or longer) plan By doing their research homework, administrators can plan staff development topics for a full year. If long periods of time are required for teachers to implement certain topics successfully, a protracted training plan for two or three years may be beneficial. As mentioned earlier, topics should be revisited, not presented as if they are being presented once for all time. For example, the following plan addresses the need for students to have more hands-on learning experiences.

Sample Staff Development Plan
ABC Christian School
Academic Year 20___ – 20___

Improvement Goals By the conclusion of the program, each teacher will be able to:
- Plan creative learning activities in each subject area that involve students in active, physically manipulative learning
- Develop lesson plans that include the efficient use of manipulative activities
- Conduct lessons that involve students in manipulative learning activities
- Evaluate learning acquired through manipulative activities

Session One (to be held on a faculty work day just prior to the start of the fall semester)
- How manipulatives affect learning
- How to integrate manipulatives into the curriculum
- How to select appropriate manipulative activities

Session Two (to be held on a "minimal" staff development day in October)
- Resources for manipulative materials
- Examples of manipulative activities in Bible, language arts skills, and mathematics

Session Three (to be held on a "minimal" staff development day in January)
- Faculty sharing of classroom experiences with manipulatives from September through December
- Faculty brainstorming of additional ideas for creating and using manipulatives

Session Four (to be held on a "minimal" day in April, followed by dinner at the administrator's home)
- How to evaluate learning generated by manipulative activities

Principle 2: Base the program on real training needs These needs can best be determined by implementing a needs-assessment process. Several suggestions for such processes are detailed later in this chapter.

Principle 3: Involve the leader(s) in training activities When administrators share in the training experience with teachers, they demonstrate that they strongly support, and believe in, the training. They also show humility when they suggest that they need the training as much as the teachers do.

Principle 4: Include a practical experience component with follow-up and individual guidance The research suggests that the most successful in-service programs include supervision and peer coaching. This individualizes the program and customizes the instruction to the needs of each teacher. Much as one-on-one tutoring instructs a child efficiently, supervision and peer coaching enable teachers to isolate their instructional problems quickly and construct the applications of new methods that best fit their particular class.

Principle 5: Structure small-group sessions Jesus worked most effectively with a group of twelve. Smaller groups permit more intense involvement, interaction, and discussion for each member than do large groups. More individual questions get answered. More individual creative ideas are voiced. More minds are more active for more of the time.

Principle 6: Make training concrete, specific, and applicable to classroom practice Each session should give teachers information or ideas they can implement immediately. If the topic is nebulous, teachers are unlikely to find the time and mental energy needed to transform theory into practice, and the training will have been largely wasted.

Principle 7: Provide released time for trainees Both early dismissals (one to two hours early) and teacher workdays prescheduled on the annual calendar qualify as released time. Teachers are more likely to participate energetically in training activities if they do not have to sacrifice time they need for grading, planning, and family responsibilities.

How Can Training Needs Be Assessed?

How can I plan a good in-service program? the Christian school administrator asks. The starting point is the faculty, since the training will benefit the teachers. The goal of the training program is to strengthen teachers in areas important to the school's instructional program. What teachers need is what the school needs, so planning must be based on the educational needs and concerns of the faculty. While input of board members and parents is important, teacher involvement will determine the program's ultimate effectiveness.

How can supervisors assess training needs? Several methods may be used:

1. **Supervisors' eyes and ears** By asking questions and discussing in-service training, supervisors can develop an informal sense of what topics are needed.

2. **Official records** By inspecting such documents as curriculum guides, unit plans, and lesson plans, supervisors and teachers may sense deficiencies that could be addressed through staff development activities.

3. **Third-party review** The administrator may call on an outside consultant, such as a Christian college professor or other trusted Christian school educator, to conduct a needs-assessment study among the school's personnel.

4. **Open-ended written survey** A short questionnaire asking teachers and supervisors their opinions of areas of need can be administered. The responses can serve to validate or repudiate data from the first three methods identified above.

5. **Check and ranking list** After a number of ideas have been gathered, a check and ranking list can be used to compile group frequency and numerical priority data.

6. **Delphi technique** This technique was developed by the Rand Corporation to forecast trends, but it can also be used in needs assessment. It combines the collection of open-ended responses with numerical or quantitative rankings. The first step is to receive open-ended comments and suggestions from teachers, reproduce all comments, and return them to all participants. Teachers read the comments and synthesize them in writing. The syntheses are then listed and duplicated for all teachers to study and rank in order of importance. The supervisor collects the rankings, computes the priorities, and returns the rankings to teachers for reranking. This procedure is repeated until certain topics appear as clear priorities.[8]

By using one or more of these procedures, administrators and teachers can identify the training topics they believe are needed most. The collaborative process creates faculty ownership of the staff development program. It is also important that the administrator be a participant, not simply a collector and dispenser of data. The administrator's thoughts and perceptions should be interjected into the planning process without short-circuiting the teachers' input. Administrators need to be pleased with the needs-assessment results. If they withdraw from the process and leave all input to teachers alone, they may not be enthusiastic about the topics that teachers identify, and the staff development plan may lack leadership and coordination.

What Faculty Gatherings Can Be Used for Staff Development?

Several kinds of faculty meetings can be used for in-service education. These include traditional after-school faculty meetings, faculty retreats, department meetings, and grade-level meetings:

Traditional after-school meeting The traditional after-school meeting has serious limitations as an in-service tool. When teachers attend such a meeting, they have been teaching all day, and ahead of them they see lessons to prepare, papers to grade, families to care for, and traffic jams to beat. The likelihood of their giving intense, productive attention to educational topics for one to two hours wanes dramatically after school dismissal time. A better alternative is to hold "minimal days" in which school is dismissed 60 to 90 minutes early. Announcing these days well in advance minimizes any inconvenience to parents.

Faculty retreat Faculty retreats permit extended attention to significant staff development topics. The retreats may take various forms: (1) a special week during the summer for which faculty are remunerated, (2) several days before school begins in the fall, or (3) prescheduled days (perhaps one per grading period) during the school year that are reserved for faculty development only.

Department or grade-level meetings These meetings allow teachers with common interests to focus on training needs applicable to their specific responsibilities. As with other faculty meetings, administrators can increase their productivity by scheduling them with concern for faculty energy levels.

How Can In-Service Sessions Be Varied?

Staff development meetings need not all be cut from the same pattern. For example, it is not always necessary to have a single presenter addressing the group. Alternative ways of dealing with instructional issues should be planned. Following are some ideas for getting faculty members involved and interested in topics under discussion.

Case studies Divide faculty into groups of four to six persons to discuss case studies of classroom situations focusing on instructional methods, management, questioning, learning modalities, or other topics.

Demonstration teaching Individual teachers or groups of teachers can demonstrate particular methods by modeling them to the entire faculty.

Microteaching Microteaching means presenting a 15- to 20-minute lesson to a small group of students (five to seven) in front of a faculty audience. Though in some ways the lesson is artificial, using school-age children adds an element of realism that demonstration teaching lacks.

Interest centers Putting new materials on display for faculty perusal allows teachers to study the innovations at their leisure. Later, the full faculty should discuss what they gleaned from the interest center displays.

Project technique Involving teachers in projects helps them to grow professionally. Projects include curriculum reviews, textbook evaluations, and evaluations of testing programs.

Role-playing Some topics such as parent conferences, student conferences, and peer supervision can be presented through role-playing by selected teachers.

Buzz groups Individual teacher participation is maximized when small groups are given topics to summarize and discuss.

Panel discussions To present new or unfamiliar information, a panel of teachers who have studied the topic may discuss what they learned at a meeting of the entire faculty.

Symposium Two speakers, representing different points of view, present a topic that is new or unfamiliar to most or all faculty members. Symposiums are presentations, not debates.

Brainstorming Brainstorming is an initial attack on a problem through the free, unlimited generation of ideas from members of the faculty. During brainstorming, group members accept all ideas without judgment. They may then generate, evaluate, rank, and classify ideas to use later in solving the problem.

Circular response When the group has more than eight to ten members and everyone's input is valued, a "circular response" structure may be employed. The entire group is seated in a circle (suggesting equality), and each member offers an opinion.

Inner-outer circles This format provides a different structure for faculty discussion of a problem or issue. The faculty is divided into two groups that are seated in concentric circles. For a specified time, the inner circle discusses the topic, with the outer circle remaining silent. The groups then exchange positions, and the former outer-circle teachers, now seated in the inner circle, have an opportunity to discuss the topic. Outer group members may be surprised at how difficult it is to keep silent and restrain themselves from injecting opinions into the inner group's discussion.

Simulation games Simulation games are activities that require participants to respond to situations as they would in life. Popular children's games like Risk, Monopoly, and Clue are simulation games. For teachers, activities like the Un-Game, in-basket problems, or case studies are useful for developing communication skills, group relationships, persuasion skills, or decision-making expertise.

Internet access during session Websites that contain information on the in-service topic under consideration may be accessed and projected for the faculty to view and discuss together. Such sites as <netdaycompass.org> are clearinghouses of teacher resource information. The equipment needed includes a computer, an in-room Internet connection, and a video projector.

Lesson modeling Madeline Hunter suggests that staff development meetings should be planned with the same care that goes into lesson planning. In-service sessions should include the essential elements of a good lesson:

Anticipatory set Developed and publicized before the meeting so that teachers know the expectations and can prepare for the learning involved.

Objectives May or may not be articulated, but are readily apparent to all participants.

Input and modeling Used as necessary. May be performed by persons, shown in a video, or presented in a publication that is distributed in advance for faculty reading. Videos of teachers in classrooms are good for modeling particular instructional techniques.

Checking for understanding Should occur at several points during the session through discussion or questions.

Guided practice Can occur when participants translate information verbally into application ideas for their own classrooms. Also may take place through follow-up supervision or peer coaching.

Independent practice Performed day after day in the classroom setting. To become permanent learning, the practice should be regular and long-term.[9]

Should Faculty Size Affect the Training Mode Selected?

Taking another approach to in-service programs, Ben Harris rated different types of activities in terms of the "experience impact" on participants. The experience impact is the degree to which each teacher is totally involved through the senses, interactions, focus, attentiveness, originality, experience control, and reality. From his ratings, the following guide to in-service activities can be structured.

Activities Effective for Small Groups	1. Structured role-playing 2. Spontaneous role-playing 3. Group therapy 4. Buzz sessions 5. Microteaching
Activities Effective for Medium-sized Groups	1. Social interaction 2. Brainstorming 3. Testing
Activities Effective for Individuals	1. Analyzing and calculating 2. Firsthand experience 3. Guided practice 4. Problem-solving interviewing 5. Therapeutic interviewing 6. Videotaping or photographing

According to Harris' evaluations, no large-group activities effectively involve participants in experience-oriented sessions. Lecturing, for instance, received the lowest score of all activities for all group sizes.[10] Still, lecturing is often the typical mode of delivery for staff development functions.

What Details Require Attention?

The most efficient needs assessment and substantive planning can be nullified if participants are hungry, uncomfortable, unable to understand, or unable to attend because of schedule conflicts. To avoid undermining the effectiveness of a potentially good in-service session, the following checklist may be used:

Meeting Preparation Checklist	
Speaker or Presenter	___ Topic clearly communicated to speaker ___ Special expectations clearly stated (time limits, group activities, etc.) ___ Speaker reconfirmed the week of the session
Facilities	___ Needed equipment on hand and working (projector, computer, etc.) ___ Public address system and acoustics in good order ___ Appropriate seating provided ___ Spare bulbs or replacement equipment on hand ___ Physical check of facility
Room Comfort	___ Heating or cooling appropriately set ___ Temperature of room (when filled) checked ___ Lighting adequate ___ Comfortable spacing between chairs
Break Times	___ Participants informed of restroom locations ___ Drinks and snacks provided ___ Participants informed of break times
Materials	___ Materials desired by leader ready ___ Distribution plan for materials prepared ___ Session evaluation forms ready for distribution[11]

The person responsible for the in-service session should be sure these details are given careful attention. Though Christian school teachers tend to be forbearing and patient, their long-suffering should not be tested unnecessarily by shoddy planning and lackluster execution of a staff development training session. In-service program planners should do everything possible to enhance the learning atmosphere for teachers, just as teachers are expected to do for students. Careful attention to detail will accomplish this goal.

What Topics Are Appropriate for In-Service Sessions?

Topics that should be treated in faculty group sessions are those that are relevant for the greatest number of teachers and are most likely to improve the school's instructional program. During the planning stages, the needs assessment should isolate these topics. The following ideas are suggested for administrators who are conducting needs assessment and prefer to give teachers some topics to consider:

Planning
1. Preparing annual course plans
2. Writing instructional objectives
3. Building unit plans
4. Constructing thematic units
5. Planning individual lessons
6. Planning interdisciplinary units/lessons
7. Planning interesting and effective Bible lessons

Integrating Biblical Principles with:
1. Natural sciences and mathematics
2. Social sciences
3. Language arts and communication skills
4. Humanities and expressive arts
5. Physical education and athletics

Delivery of Instruction
1. Using manipulatives in math
2. Teaching to a range of learning modalities and intelligences
3. Accommodating the exceptional child
4. Cooperative learning techniques
5. Grouping and individualizing instruction
6. Delivering effective whole-group instruction
7. Questioning techniques
8. Using overhead projectors
9. Teaching critical and analytical thinking
10. Effective classroom management and discipline
11. Classroom applications of computers

Evaluation
1. Writing test questions
2. Assessing writing skills
3. Using portfolio assessment techniques
4. Assessing the meaning of grades
5. How to weight grades
6. Reporting student progress to parents
7. Linking objectives to assessment

Students
1. Spiritual, physical, cognitive, and social/emotional growth stages
2. Characteristics of the learning-disabled child
3. Children from broken or single-parent homes
4. Active and attention-deficient children

Though not exhaustive, this list provides some starter topics to use in preparing an annual staff-development plan.

Chapter Summary

Group training provides administrators with alternatives to one-on-one supervision, especially when supervisor time is limited or the stimulation of group interaction is desired. Such training should be founded on biblical principles and research findings, both of which advocate training aimed at diagnosed needs.

Staff development plans should be comprehensive, need-based, experience-oriented, and applicable to classrooms. They should involve both teachers and leaders, include guidance for individual teachers, and allow released time for faculty members.

Training needs can be assessed through a variety of techniques that require faculty and administrator input. The Delphi technique is an excellent method for distilling a variety of opinions into a list of priorities.

In-service staff development sessions can take numerous formats, from lectures to small-group buzz sessions, depending on the size of the group and the training goals. Using a variety of methods injects interest into faculty meetings.

Finally, thorough attention to details and logistics will help ensure maximum effectiveness of sessions.

Supervisor's Prayer

Dear Father, Thank you for the thorough, well-planned, and individualized approach you use for our personal spiritual development. May I always let you be an example to me as I work with my faculty as a group to develop their instructional skills. Please grant me wisdom in my selection of topics and my choices of training methods. Thank you also that your Holy Spirit is the ultimate change agent in teachers' hearts. How I depend on Him to produce results in teachers' instructional approaches! To you goes all the glory for what our school is able to accomplish. In Jesus' name, Amen.

Endnotes

1. M. W. McLaughlin and D. D. Marsh, "Staff Development and School Change," *Teachers College Record* 80 (1980), 69–94.
2. J. D. Humphries, "Factors Affecting the Impact of Curriculum Innovations on Classroom Practice: Project Complexity, Characteristics of Local Leadership, and Supervisory Strategies." Unpublished doctoral dissertation, University of Georgia, 1981.
3. G. Lawrence, *Patterns of Effective In-Service Education: A State of the Art Summary of Research on Materials and Procedures for Changing Teacher Behaviors in In-Service Education,* ED 176424. Tallahassee, FL: Florida State Department of Education, 1974.
4. J. Stallings, "Allocated Academic Learning Time Revisited; or Beyond Time on Task," *Educational Researcher* 9 (1982).
5. G. G. Mohlman, "Assessing the Impact of Three In-Service Teacher Training Models," paper presented at the annual meeting of the American Educational Research Association, New York, 1982.
6. D. W. Johnson and R. T. Johnson, "Research Shows the Benefit of Adult Cooperation," *Educational Leadership* 45 (1987), 27–30.
7. Carl D. Glickman, *Supervision of Instruction: A Developmental Approach* (Boston: Allyn and Bacon, 1990), 314.
8. Ibid., 212–215.
9. Madeline Hunter and Doug Russel, *Mastery Coaching and Supervision* (El Segundo, CA: TIP Publications), 78–79.
10. Adapted from Glickman, op. cit., 329–330.
11. Ben M. Harris, *Improving Staff Performance Through In-Service Education* (Boston: Allyn and Bacon, 1980).

18

Supervision in the Small School

For who has despised the day of small things?
(Zechariah 4:10)

Chapter highlights....

Obstacles to supervision in small schools
Stretching the administrator's time
Alternative supervision techniques

Kent was a second-year Christian school administrator of a small school nestled in the mountains of Appalachia. He was also the sixth-grade teacher, soccer coach, and substitute bus driver. Because so much of Kent's time was devoted to teaching, the school's part-time secretary handled most of the administrative office duties. Special problems requiring the principal's attention were reserved for after school hours when Kent was not in class. No wonder he seemed extremely frustrated during an ACSI seminar on supervision and classroom observation techniques. During the question-and-answer session, it was Kent who asked, "How can I supervise instruction effectively when I teach sixth grade the *whole day*?"

This chapter is written for administrators like Kent. Though there are no miraculous cures for the time problems they face, there is help for administrators in small schools who want to supervise instruction effectively.

What Are the Special Obstacles to Good Supervision?

The most serious obstacle to conducting effective supervision is *lack of time*. Administrators who teach from 50 to 100 percent of the school day are seriously limited in the amount of time and the flexibility of schedule they need for classroom observation and teacher conferencing. Other tasks such as student discipline, fund-raising, and facility or vehicle maintenance absorb their attention, so that instructional supervision often receives low priority. In some schools, it is nonexistent.

Another obstacle in small schools is the *shortage of experienced educators* on the faculty. Often, the shortage is simply the result of having so few teachers. It stands to reason—the fewer the teachers, the smaller the pool of expertise from which to draw participants in such activities as peer coaching and classroom observations between teachers.

A final obstacle to effective supervision is *lack of financial resources*. Schools with small enrollments do not have adequate tuition income to support overhead expenses for teacher aides, substitutes, conference attendance or other training, and technology. Such deficiencies limit the variety and depth of instructional supervision the school can offer its faculty.

Can these obstacles be removed? The resource problem is beyond the scope of this book and, in fact, deserves a volume in itself. The rest of this chapter will address the problems of time and expertise.

What Are the Prerequisites to Solving the Time Problem?

When administrator time is consumed with actual classroom teaching, effective supervision demands a bedrock commitment to *priority* and *planning*.

However, deciding to make instructional supervision priority may be easier said than done. Despite good intentions concerning classroom observation and teacher conferencing, administrators often find themselves smothered by the "tyranny of the urgent." There is no simple solution. Belief in the importance of instructional improvement begins in the heart of the administrator. Once the conviction is embedded there, it can spread to the rest of the school constituency.

Making supervision an institutional priority Once administrators believe supervision is a necessity, they can take steps to develop schoolwide ownership of the concept. A primary way to do so is to develop and adopt a consensus *supervision policy*. Administrators are the key links in this process because they provide leadership and educational expertise for the board or pastor, and they are the ones to shepherd and develop the faculty. From this position, they can guide the board and faculty in developing a supervision policy that represents the school's commitment to instructional improvement. (For a detailed description of such a policy, see chapter 2, "The School's Supervision Policy.")

Making supervision an administrative priority Once the priority for supervision has been established, administrators can develop practical plans implementing it. (See chapter 4, "Planning for Differentiated Supervision.") Only by having a plan of action can administrators reserve time to carry out supervisory functions. Without planning and scheduling, supervision will not happen. Administrators who assume they will somehow find time for it are deceiving themselves; the "tyranny of the urgent" will inevitably exhaust that time. Proactive planning is crucial, especially in small schools where administrators have significant teaching responsibilities.

How Can Supervisory Time Be Stretched or Created?

How can Kent, the small-school administrator, have *any* time at all for supervision? At first glance, one might assume it is "mission impossible." But workable solutions exist. The following suggestions have been proposed by Christian school educators "in the trenches" who face serious time constraints in their own small-school situations.

Videotaping of class sessions for later supervisor viewing In essence, this technique reschedules the class, allowing the administrator to observe it at a time that does not conflict with other duties. Faculty members whose classes are being videotaped must understand from the start that the purpose is improvement, not judgment.

Here's how it's done. A volunteer videotapes the class. The administrator observes the tape and records supervisory notes, just as in a classroom visit, and schedules a post-observation conference. After that, the teacher keeps the videotape, assuring himself or herself that it will not be resurrected later for negative evaluation purposes. The use of videotaping in this manner allows the supervisor to teach classes as scheduled and conduct classroom observations at convenient times.

Hire substitutes to teach supervisors' classes By planning ahead, administrators can conduct several classroom observations in one day while employing substitute teachers for their own classes. The costs for the substitutes should be anticipated in the school's annual budget.

Use teacher aides to monitor supervisors' classes Teacher aides should teach only for short periods of time, not for half or full days. They can direct activities planned by the supervisor that do not require new instruction by a professional teacher. Instructional films or videotapes fit this category.

Though the use of paraprofessionals releases the supervisor to visit other classes, their overuse may leave the school open to criticism if a certificated educator is not present in the classroom.

Place supervisors' classes under other teachers' instruction This can be done when physical education, music, or art teachers are available. If the supervisor's students have one of these subjects at the same time other classes have core subjects, the supervisor can schedule visits to observe classes such as Bible, reading, and math. This idea is also feasible when the administrator's class is combined with another class under the other teacher for a single large-group lesson. For example, it may be possible to teach fifth- and sixth-graders the same Bible lessons periodically throughout the year.

Make use of the ten-to-fifteen-minute opportunities One administrator reported that she conducted numerous short, informal visits while her students were at recess, eating snacks, or on other brief breaks under adult supervision. She took short notes and gave teachers feedback even though her observation times were limited. Another limited-time activity is the "one-hour" plan described in chapter 5.

How Can Supervision Be Shared?

Administrators may implement "shared supervision" when their personal time for supervisory activities is severely limited. Shared supervision draws on the time and expertise of others.

Use a retired, experienced teacher Most communities have Christian educators who have retired from teaching. The school should consider utilizing their time and expertise by asking them to volunteer as peer supervisors to visit classes of younger teachers and give them educational counsel. Such persons sometimes receive stipends for their services. Whether paid or volunteer, they should see themselves as helpful colleagues, not authority figures.

Assign teachers as "buddies," or peer supervisors This strategy allows teachers to share their experience and insight with each other through observing and counseling. (For more detail, see chapter 9, "Tools for Teacher Self-Improvement.") Teachers may visit their buddies' classrooms personally or by reviewing videotaped sessions. Either way, they should share their insights promptly in a follow-up conference. Buddies report their progress to each other and the school administrator.

Require considerable videotaping and teacher self-analysis The faculty and administrator may set up a plan in which teachers arrange for three or four class videotapings per semester. Teachers then conduct a self-analysis using the same format that supervisors would use if they visited classes personally. The missing ingredient, of course, is the input of an experienced outsider. It is the rare teacher who can self-critique with total objectivity.

Hold group supervision sessions Group supervision allows discussion of topics of common need or interest to all teachers. These sessions do not conflict with teaching schedules, nor do they require teaching administrators to be absent from their own classes. Various forms of in-service training are discussed in chapter 17, "Group Techniques in Supervision."

Draw on expertise of other Christian schools Small schools that are geographically near larger, more mature Christian schools may consider an interschool supervision agreement. Here is how such an arrangement might work. First, the small school needs educational expertise not currently available in its staff. It arranges with a school that has knowledgeable Christian educators on its staff for periodic visits from those master teachers. The purpose is to provide peer supervision and classroom observations for the small school. To defray expenses, the small school pays stipends to the larger school for substitutes while its teachers are absent for cross-supervision activities.

Chapter Summary

There are no "quick fixes" for the supervision constraints faced by small-school administrators who teach a good portion of the school day. The starting point is to obtain institutional commitment, from board to faculty, for giving high priority to instructional supervision. Once this commitment has been made, careful planning of time and personnel can make adequate supervision possible.

There are two approaches to practicing supervision in small schools. One is for supervisors to find time during the day when they can observe teachers' classes. Various methods can be employed to create the necessary time. The second approach is to make use of other resources and expertise for giving teachers guidance on instructional improvement, allowing the administrator to continue a regular teaching schedule. The best solution for a particular school is to tailor a plan that best meets its own needs, often by combining aspects of both approaches.

Regardless of how a school decides to meet its supervision needs, the administrator must lead in the advance planning of schedules and the advance budgeting of necessary funds. In other words, once a school is committed to making supervision a priority, only specific, concrete, thoughtful planning can assure it will actually happen.

Supervisor's Prayer

Dear Father in Heaven, I thank you that you have told us to "despise not the day of small beginnings." We are also reminded that you gave special attention to a group of twelve men. Therefore, we thank you for the special place smallness has in your great kingdom work. Now I ask for your Spirit to multiply and bless the efforts of small-school administrators and faculty members, especially as they seek to make their schools a testimony to your excellence. We will praise you for the results. Through our Savior we pray, Amen.

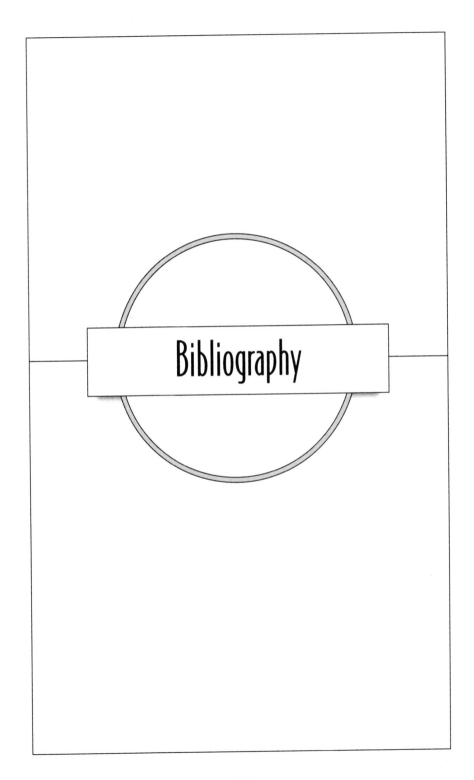

Bibliography

Abrami, Philip C. et al. "The Relationship Between Student Personality Characteristics, Teacher Ratings, and Student Achievement." *Journal of Educational Psychology* 74 (1982).

Acheson, Keith A. and Meredith Damien Gall. *Techniques in the Clinical Supervision of Teachers.* New York: Longman, 1997.

Albrecht, Judith D. et al. "A Comparison of High School Student Ratings of Teacher Effectiveness with Teacher Self-Ratings: Factor Analytic and Multitrait-Multimethod Analysis." *Educational and Psychological Measurement* 46 (1986).

Blair, Julie. "Cincinnati Teachers to Be Paid on Performance." *Education Week* (27 September 2000).

Blome. Unpublished study reported in "Principles of Supervision," chapter by A. C. Fortosis in Roy W. Lowrie, ed. *Administration of the Christian School.* Colorado Springs: Association of Christian Schools International, 1984.

Blumberg, Arthur and William Greenfield. *The Effective Principal: Perspectives on School Leadership.* Boston, MA: Allyn and Bacon, 1980.

Brown, Gordon B. *Leader Behavior and Faculty Cohesiveness in Christian Schools.* Doctoral dissertation. Miami, FL: University of Miami, 1982.

————. Unpublished survey conducted at Grace Theological Seminary, Winona Lake, IN, 1990.

————. From "Supervision of Instruction," an ACSI-sponsored seminar, 2000.

Carney, Burt, ed. *Christian School Personnel Forms.* Colorado Springs, CO: Association of Christian Schools International, 2001.

Cogan, Morris L. *Clinical Supervision.* Boston: Houghton Mifflin, 1973.

Deci, E. L. "Motivation." Paper presented to the annual meeting of the Midwest Association of Teachers of Educational Psychology, Dayton, OH, 1982.

Dull, Lloyd W. *Supervision: School Leadership Handbook.* Columbus, OH: Merrill Publishing Company, 1981.

Eisner, E. W. *The Educational Imagination: On the Design and Evaluation of School Programs.* 2d ed. New York, NY: MacMillan, 1985.

Fagan, Michael M. and Glen Walter. "Mentoring Among Teachers." *The Journal of Educational Research* 76 (1982).

Fortosis, A. C. "Principles of Supervision," chapter in *Administration of the Christian School* (Roy W. Lowrie, Jr., ed.). Colorado Springs, CO: Association of Christian Schools International, 1984.

Gersten, Russell and Douglas Carnine. *Administrative and Supervisory Support Functions for the Implementation of Effective Educational Programs for Low Income Students.* Eugene, OR: Center for Educational Policy and Management, University of Oregon, 1981.

Glatthorn, Allan A. *Differentiated Supervision.* Alexandria, VA: Association for Supervision and Curriculum Development, 1997.

Glickman, Carl D. *Supervision of Instruction: A Developmental Approach.* 2d ed. Boston: Allyn and Bacon, 1990.

Glickman, Carl D., Stephen P. Gordon, and Jovita M. Ross-Gordon. *Supervision of Instruction: A Developmental Approach.* 4th ed. Boston: Allyn and Bacon, 1998.

Goldhammer, Robert, Robert H. Anderson, and Robert J. Krajewski. *Clinical Supervision.* 2d ed. New York: Holt, Rinehart, Winston, 1980.

Hanna, Gerald S. et al. "Discriminant and Convergent Validity of High School Student Ratings of Instruction." *Educational and Psychological Measurement* 43 (1983).

Harris, Ben M. *Improving Staff Performance Through In-service Education.* Boston: Allyn and Bacon, 1980.

———. *Supervisory Behavior in Education.* Englewood Cliffs, NJ: Prentice-Hall, 1963.

Harris, Ben M. et al. *Personnel Administration in Education.* Boston: Allyn and Bacon, 1979.

Harris, Laurie. "Teacher Evaluations: How to Observe and Conference for Results" (Tape 1). Produced for the International Fellowship of Christian School Administrators, 1998.

Hersey, Paul and Kenneth Blanchard. *Management of Organizational Behavior: Utilizing Human Resources.* Englewood Cliffs, NJ: Prentice-Hall, 1982.

Hertzberg, F., B. Mauser, and B. Snyderman. *The Motivation to Work.* New York: Wiley, 1959.

Hoy, Wayne and Cecil Miskel. *Educational Administration: Theory, Research, Practice.* New York: McGraw-Hill, 1991.

Humphries, J. D. *Factors Affecting the Impact of Curriculum Innovations on Classroom Practice: Project Complexity, Characteristics of Local Leadership, and Supervisory Strategies,* unpublished doctoral dissertation, University of Georgia, 1981.

Hunter, Madeleine and Doug Russell. *Mastery Coaching and Supervision.* El Segundo, CA: TIP Publications.

Hyman, Ronald T. *School Administrator's Faculty Supervision Handbook.* Englewood Cliffs, NJ: Prentice-Hall, 1986.

Johnson, D. W. and R. T. Johnson. "Research Shows the Benefit of Adult Cooperation." *Educational Leadership* 45 (1987).

Knoll, Marcia. *Supervision for Better Instruction.* Englewood Cliffs, NJ: Prentice-Hall, 1987.

Lawrence, G. *Patterns of Effective In-service Education: A State of the Art Summary of Research on Materials and Procedures for Changing Teacher Behaviors in In-service Education.* Tallahassee, FL: Florida State Department of Education, 1974.

Maslow, Abraham H. *Motivation and Personality.* New York: Harper and Row, 1954.

McFaul, Shirley A. and James M. Cooper. "Peer Clinical Supervision in an Urban Elementary School." *Journal of Teacher Education* 34 (1983).

McLaughlin, M. W. and D. D. Marsh. "Staff Development and School Change." *Teachers College Record* 80 (1) (1978).

Mertler, Craig A. "Students as Stakeholders in Teacher Evaluation: Teacher Perceptions of a Formative Feedback Model." Paper presented at the annual meeting of the Midwestern Educational Research Association (Chicago, IL, October 15–18, 1997).

Mohlman, G. G. "Assessing the Impact of Three In-service Teacher Training Models." Paper presented at the annual meeting of the American Educational Research Association (New York, 1982).

The New Teacher's Guide to the U.S. Department of Education, September 1997, cited 29 December 2000; available from <http://www.ed.gov/pubs/TeachersGuide/teach.html>.

Oakley, Timothy. "Supervision Through Videotaping." Paper prepared at Grace Theological Seminary, Winona Lake, IN (1991).

Pajak, Edward. *Approaches to Clinical Supervision: Alternatives for Improving Instruction* Norwood, MA: Christopher-Gordon Publishers, 2000.

Pathwise Software: A Framework for Teaching. Princeton, NJ: Educational Testing Service, 1998.

Richards, Lawrence O. and Clyde Hoeldtke. *A Theology of Church Leadership.* Grand Rapids, MI: Zondervan, 1980.

Rush, Myron. *Management: A Biblical Approach.* Wheaton, IL: Victor Books, 1984. [Reprinted in 2002 by Chariot Victor, Colorado Springs, CO.]

Schain, Robert L. *Supervising Instruction: What It Is and How to Do It.* Brooklyn, NY: Educators Practical Press, 1988.

Sergiovanni, Thomas J. "Why Should We Seek Substitutes for Leadership?" *Educational Leadership* 49 (5) (1992).

Sheppard, B. "Exploring the Transformational Nature of Instructional Leadership." *The Alberta Journal of Educational Research* 42 (1996).

Stallings, J. "Allocated Academic Learning Time Revisited, or Beyond Time on Task." *Educational Researcher* 9 (11) (1980).